STORIES
OF
GOD
An Unauthorized Biography
by
John Shea

STORIES
OF
GOD

An Unauthorized Biography

by
John Shea

THE THOMAS MORE PRESS
Chicago, Illinois

The author wishes to thank the following for permission to incorporate in his text:

Excerpts from *The Jerusalem Bible*, copyright © 1966 by Darton, Longman & Todd, Ltd. and Doubleday & Company, Inc. Used by permission of the publisher.

Quotation from *The Marriage Feast* by Par Lagerkvist, translated by Alan Blair. Copyright © 1954 by Albert Bonniers Forlag. Reprinted with the permission of Farrar, Straus & Giroux, Inc.

Quotations from *Report to Greco* by Nikos Kazantzakis, copyright © 1965 by the author and *St. Francis* by Nikos Kazantzakis, copyright © 1962 by the author. Reprinted by permission of Simon & Schuster, Inc.

Quotation from *Messengers of God: Biblical Portraits and Legends* by Elie Wiesel, copyright © 1976 by the author. Reprinted by permission of Random House, Inc.

Quotation from *The Gates of the Forest* by Elie Wiesel, copyright © 1966 by the author. Reprinted by permission of the publishers, Holt, Rinehart & Winston, Inc.

Lines from *You Can't Go Home Again* by Thomas Wolfe, © 1934 by the author. Reprinted by permission of Harper & Row, Inc.

Lines from *Mass* by Leonard Bernstein. Copyright Leonard Bernstein. Printed by permission of G. Schirmer, Inc., New York.

Sixth Printing

ISBN: 0-88347-085-3

CONTENTS

Preface

When the great Rabbi Israel Baal Shem-Tov saw misfortune threatening the Jews it was his custom to go into a certain part of the forest to meditate. There he would light a fire, say a special prayer, and the miracle would be accomplished and the misfortune averted.

Later, when his disciple, the celebrated Magid of Mezeritch, had occasion, for the same reason, to intercede with heaven, he would go to the same place in the forest and say: "Master of the Universe, listen! I do not know how to light the fire, but I am still able to say the prayer." And again the miracle would be accomplished.

Still later, Rabbi Moshe-Leib of Sassov, in order to save his people once more, would go into the forest and say: "I do not know how to light the fire, I do not know the prayer, but I know the place and this must be sufficient." It was sufficient and the miracle was accomplished.

Then it fell to Rabbi Israel of Rizhin to overcome misfortune. Sitting in his armchair, his head in his hands, he spoke to God: I cannot even find the place in the forest. All I can do is to tell the story, and this must be sufficient." And it was sufficient.

God made man because he loves stories.

—Elie Wiesel
The Gates of the Forest

IF GOD made man because he loves stories, creation is a success. For humankind is addicted to stories. No matter our mood, in reverie or expectation, panic or peace, we can be found

stringing together incidents, and unfolding episodes. We turn our pain into narrative so we can
bear it; we turn our ecstasy into narrative so we
can prolong it. We all seem to be under the sen-
tence of Scheherazade. We tell our stories to live.

But there is a deeper suggestion in Wiesel's
phrase. God not only loves to hear our stories, he
loves to tell his own. And, quite simply, *we* are
the story God tells. Our very lives are the words
that come from his mouth. This insight has
always fired the religious imagination, refusing to
be rationalized or dismissed. The conviction that
we are God's story releases primordial impulses
and out of a mixture of beligerence, gratitude,
and imitation we return the compliment. We tell
stories of God.

Someone has outlined the perennial Christian
strategy as:

1. Gather the folks.
2. Break the bread.
3. Tell the stories.

This book explores the stories the folks tell when
they gather to break the bread. As Christians we
have inherited ancient stories that carry the faith
convictions of our people Although these stories
may start with "long ago," they end with "right
now." There is an enduring world-creating
ability to the stories of God. This book hopes to
enter into some of those possible worlds. Although this book relies on scholarship, it is not a
scholarly work. Although in places it summarizes,

it is not a popular summary. It is a book about understanding the stories of God so that when we tell them, they will be "sufficient."

Before telling the stories of God, we must understand ourselves as storytellers. The first chapter attempts to describe the human situation in such a way that it becomes a natural locale for the stories of God. These stories are not aliens, smuggled into human life, but the inevitable companions of people bounded by birth and death. In short, since we are inescapably related to Mystery, we inescapably talk about it. The second chapter explores what the stories of God do for us when we tell them. To tell a story of God is to create a world, adopt an attitude, suggest a behavior. But stories are first; we are second. We are born into a community of stories and storytellers. In interpreting our traditional stories of God we find out who we are and what we must do. In telling the stories of God we ourselves are told.

Chapters three to five weave the established Christian symbols into stories of God. They do not concentrate on specific stories, e.g., Moses bargaining with God in the desert. Instead they try to surface and clarify the overall pattern of the God-Humankind relationship. First, the symbols of rescue and covenant, judgment and apocalypse, resurrection and parousia are interrelated to tell a story of hope and justice. Secondly, the symbols of creation, incarnation, spirit and fall, crucifixion, church — separate and merge to tell a story of trust and freedom. These two stories, or sets of stories, establish the content and values of a Christian world. The last story of invitation and decision describes the redemptive process of this Christian world. Together they tell a rounded story of God which, of course, is a rounded story of us.

There are many people to thank. To my family— John and Ann, Gail and Len, Barbara and Tom— who "put up" with me while I hibernated. To Thomas More Press who waited while I worked— off schedule. Especially to Rita, whose ceaseless typewriter is the story of this book.

Whatever else can be said of the evangelist of the fourth Gospel, he knew how to end. "There were many other things that Jesus did; if all were written down, the world itself, I suppose, would not hold all the books that would have to be written." His ending is this book's beginning. Inside are a few of the stories that Christians tell, a few of the worlds they inhabit, a few of the fears that attack them, a few of the tasks that intrigue them, a few of the invitations that lure them, a few of the decisions that face them.

There are many more.

CHAPTER ONE
Exceeding Darkness and Undeserved Light

Religion . . . elaborates on what feels profoundly true even though it is not demonstrable; it translates into significant words, images, and codes the exceeding darkness which surrounds man's existence, and the light which pervades it beyond all desert or comprehension.[1]

—Erik Erikson

IN THE MATTER of human existence the grave and sensible advice of the King of Hearts—"Begin at the beginning"—cannot be heeded. We have no choice but to begin where we are; and where we are is the middle. It is not given us to stand on the far side of human space, at a moment before the rush of human time and then, with all deliberation and grace, to enter. Nor is it given us to find an indisputable starting point, a Cartesian rock from which to launch understanding and action. Our first awareness is that we are swimming. We wake in the water. Our beginnings are not wholly our own. Our endings will most likely be beyond our control. We are middle people.

As middle people we are caught, in William James' phrase, in the "particular go" of things; or put more graphically, in "booming, buzzing, confusion." Our experiences are the turns of a kaleidoscope, technicolor patterns dissolving and

reconfiguring. Impressions are too numerous to
record, thoughts too fleeting to assimilate. Feelings rock us and our rational actions turn impul-
sive and unmanageable. In this sound and fury
we need a perspective, an angle of vision. We do
not seek a mountaintop from which to cynically
eye the human drama or a cultivated sloth that
cannot hear what Kazantzakis called a Great Cry
"blowing through heaven and earth, and in our
hearts and in the heart of every living thing."[2]
What we seek is a way to explore all that we are
and can become, to understand enough to savor
the richness and stare straight into the pain. The
psychiatrist in Peter Shaffer's play *Equus* says it
simply, "I need a way of seeing in the dark."

But before we tell our stories (which is the human way of seeing) we must explore the basic
contours of our existence, the exceeding darkness
and undeserved light. For these are the sub-
stratum of all story, the elements of the human
condition which keep us telling our tales long into
the night.

Although the concrete flow of each life is indis-
putably unique, it is also undeniably similar. We
all share a common set of environments. The
self, family and friends, society and institution,
and universe are relationships which no human
life escapes.[3] The human biography unfolds in the
rich and intricate interweaving of the self and
these multiple environments. Yet the fact that we
have a biography at all reveals another relatedness, a relatedness which suffuses yet trans-

cends these environments. This relationship is more elusive than the others and often goes unacknowledged. But when it bursts into consciousness (and that is how it usually enters), it rivets the psyche and its importance is beyond question. We are inescapably related to Mystery.

Our most immediate and in many ways our most baffling environment is ourselves. We are capable of everyday yet always bizarre remarks like, "There I go—being defensive again," or "I'm learning to live with myself," or the poignant comment of a retarded girl, "I'm not so dumb I don't know I'm stupid." We are able—and many say this is the distinctively human thing—to remove ourselves from ourselves to see how we are doing with ourselves. This reflexive ability is never far from any human endeavor. In Bernard Malamud's *The Fixer*, Yakov is on his way to a woman's bed.

> Should I stay or should I go? Yakov thought. On the one hand its been a long season without rain. A man is not a man for nothing. What do the Hasidim say? "Hide not from thine own flesh." On the other hand what does this mean to me? At my age it is nothing new. It means nothing."[4]

As far as we know, we are the only animals who debate about sex. We talk to ourselves and so set up a relationship which, while not schizophrenic, makes a simple animal reaction to stimuli impossible.

A second environment is family and friends,

those people who are continually near us and with whom there is sustained interaction. Our contact with them is intimate and personal. Our lives and theirs flow into each other; their fortunes and failures affect us. This environment is the primary locale of human development and the setting of our most lively hopes and our most persistent fears. We search here for fulfillment and security and we fear that if we fail here, we fail as human beings. Intimacy or isolation, love or loneliness are the qualities which are generated in the environment of interpersonal relationships.

A third environment of the self is society and its institutions. We are more than our own privacy and our circle of family and friends. We belong to a race, city, nation, Church and world. This relatedness, although not always as immediate as the interpersonal, is powerfully, and often covertly, influential. Society and institution assign roles, grant legitimacy or illegitimacy to certain behavior, control the means of production, and provide sanctions, as Michael Novak has said, "from raised eyebrows to death penalties." Whether we view society and institution as repressive constructs or the creative matrix of all human action, they form an inescapable environment of life.

A fourth environment is the non-human universe. The universe is more than a stage and props for the human drama. The resources of the earth are vital to the well-being of human society and if at times we are tempted to forget this, an ecological crisis painfully reminds us. Also our physical environment influences our psychic make-up. The weather depresses or cheers us and more than one poet has written of the land which shapes our basic self-image. Chesterton once remarked that he never understood the gods of Norse mythology until he saw the low, brooding skies of Scandinavia. We, in turn, through technological prowess have changed our physical surroundings. We have created lakes and canals, made forests into farmlands and plains into cities. In recent times this manipulation of the earth has raised serious problems. Humankind is in a continuous and, what has become increasingly obvious, highly dangerous interaction with the non-human universe.

Alfred North Whitehead has remarked that experience is one of the most deceitful words in philosophy. But perhaps a broad definition might be derived from this brief sketch. Human experiencing is the reciprocal flow between the self and its environments. On the one hand we do not passively receive or mechanically react to stimuli from our environments. We do more than register the results. We interpret what we receive according to symbolic structures of our mind. The Thomistic maxim is valid: "Whatever is received is received according to the mode of the receiver." On the other hand we do not arbitrarily interpret what has been received. We interpret in patterns which the input from our environments suggest. In the matter of human experience it is misleading to speak of merely subjective or strictly objective. Human experience is dynamic interrelating.

In the immediate past, experience was often very narrowly conceived, limited to what the senses were capable of delivering. Today it is understood as the pervasive atmosphere of all human development. We are not fully formed people who, as an afterthought, move outward. Our relationships with our environments are not "something" we have but "something" through which we come to be. Our experiences are constitutive of who we are, not extras which we could well do without. Henry James' description may be overblown but it brings home the importance and all embracing nature of experience.

> Experience is never limited, and it is never complete; it is an immense sensibility, a kind of huge spiderweb of the finest silken threads suspended in the chamber of consciousness, and catching every air-borne particle in its tissue. It is the very atmosphere of the mind.[5]

The human person could be defined as the sum of his experiences, the complex of his relationships with his own self, others, society and universe.

But there is more, a distinctive and very important more. Human experiencing reveals another relatedness. This relatedness is not a fifth environment but a dimension present and available in every environment. In psychological jargon it is not a field, but a field encompassing field. It is not experienced separately but is encountered as the depth of every interaction of the self and its environments. This dimension is referred to in many ways. It has been called the Transcendent, the Ultimate, the Sacred, the More, the Whole, the Encompassing, the Inexhaustible, Being. These words are not so much names which define this reality but acknowledgments of its presence. They are attempts to focus on what is so pervasive and so near that it often goes uncelebrated. This transcendent yet permeating reality we will call the dimension of Mystery.

The process of becoming aware of the dimension of Mystery differs from both mysticism and rationalism. The mystical experience connotes a sense of immediacy, an intense merger with Mystery. The desire is for a pure, unencumbered communion. The everyday environments of the self are leapt over and left behind. They are not vehicles for contact with Mystery but, if anything, obstacles. In this sense, mysticism is concerned with special religious experience and not the religious dimension of ordinary human experience. The rationalistic approach, on the other hand, initially concentrates on immediate environments. In fact, it begins with some indisputable datum of experience. But once grounded in experience, it begins to stepladder toward an inevitable transcendence. The process is one of logical inference, showing that if this is the case, then this also must be the case. If there is such a thing as motion, in the famous Thomistic argument, then many logical links later there must be an Unmoved Mover. Both mysticism and rationalism approach Mystery by moving away from ordinary experience.

A middle way, between mystical rapture and lock-step proof and the one which seems both the richest and the most available, is the way of sacrament and feeling. Everyday awareness has two points. For example, I (1) see a bird (2). Sacramental awareness has three points—I (1) see a bird (2) and in and through this interaction become aware of the dimension of Mystery (3). Gerard Manly Hopkins sees a windhover fighting the currents of the wind and in his struggle he is plunged into the mystery of human redemption. Two people are in love; and in their love for each other they become aware of a larger love in which they participate, the source of their own care. This is sacramental awareness. Unlike mysticism it does not bypass our immediate environments but goes through them. Unlike rational awareness it does not engage in an extensive logical process. Mystery enters into consciousness as the premise of life not the conclusion of logic. The sacramental way is the way of the poet and novelist. Perhaps Flannery O'Connor's language is most suggestive. We discover Mystery through manners and our true country (what is eternal) through the contours of our ordinary countryside.

Feeling is the way we perceive the dimension of Mystery. A popular misunderstanding of feeling reduces it to emotionality. But feeling is both cognitive and affective. It is the way in which the total person appropriates Whole or Mystery or Encompassing. Since the dimension of Mystery, in Gilkey's phrase, "is not so much seen but the basis of seeing; not what is known as an object so much as the basis of knowing; not an object of value but the ground of valuing; not the thing before us but the source of things; not the particular meanings that generate our life in the world but the ultimate context within which these meanings necessarily subsist,"[6] it is not observed and detected like individual objects. Feeling perceives by participation. It cannot observe from the outside for there is no outside. It cannot step back for a "better look" for there is quite literally no place to go. There is no vantage point from which to spy on Mystery. Since it is the permeating context of all being and activity, all perception is from within. We are intimately involved and our awareness of that involvement comes through a feeling perception which engages the entire person.

An insight from Martin Heidegger and another from Mircea Eliade might help explore the sacramentality of our awareness of Mystery. It is either the great strength or great liability of Heidegger's thought that his insights seem inseparable from his vocabulary. In Heideggerian argot all reality is constructed of Being-beings. Beings are all objects which are available to the procedures of practical and theoretical approaches. Being is the "to be" of whatever is, the power which makes beings possible. Being and beings are distinct but never separable. A being is never without Being for Being makes beings possible. On the other hand Being is never without beings for Being only reveals itself, if it does at all, through beings. Therefore, an awareness of beings, the surface of reality, can bring with it awareness of Being, the depth of reality. Heidegger's meditation on a pair of peasant shoes in a Van Gogh painting brings out this relationship.

> From the dark opening of the worn insides of the shoes the toilsome tread of the worker stares forth. In the stiffly rugged heaviness of the shoes there is the accumulated tenacity of her slow trudge through the far-spreading and ever-uniform furrows of the field swept by a raw wind. On the leather lie the dampness and richness of the soil. Under the soles slides the loneliness of the field-path as evening falls. In the shoes vibrates the silent call of the earth, its quiet gift of the ripening grain and its unexplained self-refusal in the fallow desolation of the wintry field. This equipment is pervaded by uncomplaining anxiety as to the certainty of bread, the wordless joy of having once more withstood want, the trembling before the impending childbed and shivering at the surrounding menace of death. This equipment belongs to the *earth*, and it is protected in the *world* of the peasant woman. . . . Being, as presence, emerges through the painting of the shoes; yet in such a way that it enfolds them in their concrete thingness—just a pair of shoes, and nothing else—as the simple, serviceable gear that they are.[7]

The Heideggerian awareness of Being helps to illuminate the sacramental awareness of Mystery.

A similar view of sacramentality is contained in Eliade's notion of the multivalent nature of religious language. The primary characteristic of religious language is that it has a double referent. It refers to both a concrete "object" and the transcendent dimension which manifests itself through that "object." Religious language talks about a pearl, a mountain, a historical event, a book, a people but only insofar as they mediate transcendent reality. For example, religious language about the crucifixion of Jesus is more than a historical reconstruction of what happened. It is talk about that event in relation to the Sacred that appeared within it. Sacramental consciousness does not desert the concrete, historical world but turns it to symbol. It is sensitive to every experience for all human interaction is capable of becoming revelatory. Hierophany, a manifestation of the Sacred, may be the next moment. In a striking analogy Eliade stresses the hierophanic nature of the world for the primitive person and its opacity for modern people. "We have only to imagine a communion, no longer limited to the eucharistic elements of bread or wine, but extending to every kind of 'substance,' in order to measure the distance separating a primitive religious experience from the modern experience of 'natural phenomena'."[8]

Eliade's sentiments about contemporary religious experience are frequently echoed. It is often said that the sacramentality of human relating, its transparency to Mystery, is particularly difficult to experience today. The modern person is blocked, entrapped in two-point awareness, unable to touch the dimension of Mystery. The alleged cause of this blockage is the technological spirit which encourages endless manipulation of the surface of reality but is insensitive to its depth. In some cases the success of science and the pervasiveness of technology has had this sad side-effect. Secular scientific consciousness becomes the only way the human person relates to reality. Only those aspects of human existence which fit within the narrow canons of scientific truth and method are granted reality. All else is meaningless and false. In this situation, as Heidegger suggests, Being is forgotten. Mark Twain, having learned the technicalities of piloting a steamboat down the Mississippi, knew the problem:

> Now when I had mastered the language of this water, and had come to know every trifling feature that bordered the great river as familiarly as I knew the letters of the alphabet, I had made a valuable acquisition. But I had lost something, too. I had lost something which could never be restored to me while I lived. All the grace, and beauty, the poetry, had gone out of the majestic river! . . . All the value any feature of it had for me now was the amount of usefulness it could furnish toward compassing the safe piloting of a steamboat.[9]

The consistent neglect of the dimension of Mystery, and the sensitivity to the givenness of things which is brings, stunts the possibilities of being human. It reduces the ranges of human consciousness and can produce a person who "seems to be possessed by a rebellion against human existence as it has been given, a free gift from nowhere (secular speaking) which he wishes to exchange as it were, for something he has made himself."[10]

But is this really the choice? Are we caught in the dilemma—either the river is the path of Mystery or the path to New Orleans?

Although it is true that the scientific spirit has often obscured the sacramental character of experience, it is not an unalterable foe of religious consciousness. In the 17th and 18th centuries an understanding of the givenness of the physical universe was the motivation and rationale for serious scientific inquiry. The fact that the world had been created by a Divine Intellect meant that its ways were intelligible. And since the human person also possessed an intellect, he was capable of discovering these ways and harnessing them for the betterment of humankind. It is one of the strange ironies of the history of science and religion that the very God who encouraged scientific inquiry was eventually discredited by it. But no matter what theological or philosophical conceptualization it may take—an awareness of "the givenness of things" which makes us sensitive to the dimension of Mystery is not an obstacle to scientific advance. In fact, Einstein believed this awareness was the source of all science and art. "The most beautiful thing we can experience is the mysterious side of life. It is the deep feeling which is at the cradle of all true art and science. In this sense, and only in this sense, I count myself amongst the most deeply religious people."[11]

Conversely, scientific advance does not render the world opaque but, from a certain mind-set, increases its sacramentality. The discoveries of science do not encroach on the dimension of Mystery. The exploration of space may demolish the mythological home of God but we are not left with an impoverished universe but with a more wondrous one. Endless space may cut into our conceptualizations but it heightens rather than diminishes our sense of Mystery. The future relationship of science and religious consciousness may be one of those reversals which historians love to point out. The very endeavor—science and technology—which at one stage of history obscured the religious dimension of human existence at another stage will discover it on its own terms and with its own nuances. Science does not threaten to exhaust transcendence but reaffirms it in every advance.

Although the technological spirit does not mean automatic insensitivity to Mystery, we do live in an age tempted to a secular restriction of consciousness. This temptation is often caricatured as the flat-earth impulse, the tendency to level all vertical awareness to a horizontal understanding. Anything that smacks of transcendence is immediately flattened. All relation to God is translated without remainder into a relation with our neighbor. In the face of this reductionistic tendency some of the paths to an awareness of Mystery must be mapped.

The ways to this awareness of the ultimate dimension of human experience are myriad. It is not an exaggeration to say that no two people travel the same path. Yet Simone Weil's observation might apply—we travel different paths through the forest but come upon the same clearing. An old man sits by the sea and knows that the waves he watches will crash on those shores long after he is gone. He is triggered into an awareness of the Mystery within which both he and the waves dwell. A young mother watches her child at the park and suddenly wonder seizes her and carries her into an awareness of Mystery. The car just ahead of us spins off the road and crashes down the embankment. We say we were lucky but wonder why; and the persistent question pushes us into the dimension of Mystery. We are related not only to the sea, the child, the highway but to the Mystery which both contextualizes and suffuses those environments.

A fundamental human experience which often carries us to the awareness of Mystery is contingency, what Kazantzakis calls the luminous interval between two darknesses. The story that opens the Dutch Catechism is worth retelling.

> In A.D. 627 the monk Paulinus visited King Edwin in northern England to persuade him to accept Christianity. He hesitated and decided to summon his advisers. At the meeting one of them stood up and said: 'Your majesty, when you sit at table with your lords and vassals, in the winter when the fire burns warm and bright on the hearth and the storm is howling outside, bringing the snow and the rain, it happens of a sudden that a little bird flies into the hall. It comes in at one door and flies out through the other. For the few moments that it is inside the hall, it does not feel the cold, but as soon as it leaves your sight, it returns to the dark of winter. It seems to me that the life of man is much the same. We do not know what went before and we do not know what follows. If the new doctrine can speak to us surely of these things, it is well for us to follow it.'

When we meditate on our coming and going, we are forced to ask the meaning of it all and the awareness of Mystery is upon us. And if we follow the strange lead to our heart and imagination, we are soon in ontological wonder—"Why is there anything at all?"

At times we experience our contingency in a positive way.[12] There are days when the sun is within us, when the joy of just being alive pulses through us. We exult in the very fact that we are and marvel at our powers and sensations. This joy in being alive is often unconscious, an underlying tone to our vitality. But there are moments when it bursts into consciousness: "God, it's good to be alive!" These moments of exultation, when the power of life seizes us, come to us unbidden. They suddenly shoot through us, erupt within us. We are not able by a grunt of our will to bring about this experience; and when we try, it strikes us as forced and unreal. The experience is a gift.

The athlete knows the gifts contingent existence can bring. He trains; he tunes his body and spirit to perform with speed and accuracy. Yet one game he is "off." Every move is too slow, every effort ineffective. Another game he is "on." "When you're hot, you're hot," the slogan goes. Everything is in sync. And although he has trained for this moment, more than training is present. He feels the power of life surging through him, expressing itself in his grace and precision. The mother giving birth also knows this unbidden gift of power. In the process of birth she is no longer her own. The contractions start and the power of life will have its way. She becomes the symbol of the mysterious and the wonderful. She is in as intimate a union as anyone ever is with the Mystery of Life.

Yet not far from this experience of positive contingency, the exhilarating awareness that life is given, is the anxious awareness that it is not guaranteed. No insurance policy can quite tame the future. Death and all its lesser indignities— illness, suffering, and loss—await us. All our devices to make life safe—amassing money and military might—are ultimately only stalls. Our meanings are fragile, our loves passing, our hopes precarious. When the reliability of all we have constructed is brought into question, we enter the dimension of Mystery. We wonder what it all means. The fast answers that our immediate environments give are no longer seductive. We look beyond into Mystery. Thomas Wolf once looked beyond, beautifully:

> To lose the earth you know, for greater knowing;
> to lose the life you have, for greater life;
> to leave the friends you loved, for greater loving;
> to find a land more kind than home, more large than earth . . . Whereon the pillars of this earth are founded, towards which the consciousness of the world is tending—a wind is rising, and the river flow.[13]

Although the experience of contingency is probably the most traveled path, the awareness of Mystery is often present in two activities which constitute human selfhood—dialogue and communion. Gregory Baum has carefully mapped this path to Mystery.[14] The human person comes to be through dialogue with others. Out of this ongoing dialogue a person develops a sense of who she is and where she is going. People speak to each other words of acceptance and love but they also speak painful words that call for conversion and new life-styles. For Baum, in and through these words a special word is spoken. A word which transcends the people involved. The word is discerned as transcendent and gratuitous because the speaker knows that it is not necessarily hers alone and that by it she herself is judged.

The same awareness is present in communion. A person in communion with other people is loved and accepted. In this love and acceptance she finds the strength to reply to the special word of conversion offered her. This love and acceptance which is the core of a person's freedom is a gift given to her by others. But here again a person senses that the gift of human communion goes beyond itself. She intuits that the gift dimension of life is more than she is. Sensitivity to depth of dialogue and communion often facilitates the awareness of Mystery.

Another path to Mystery is collapse. When order crumbles, Mystery rises. When our most prized assumptions about life are suddenly ripped from us, Mystery appears as a fury which threatens to engulf us. No protective symbols are available, no interpretive culture buffers its impact on the human soul. Its appearance is frightening; its name is the abyss. For many in the twentieth century it is this chaotic face of Mystery which has revealed itself. Par Lagerkvist in *My Father and I* has seen it. When Lagerkvist was a small boy, he and his father went for a walk on Sunday afternoon. It was a beautiful day and their walk took them farther than they expected. Suddenly it was night and they were engulfed in darkness. In order to find their way they followed the railroad tracks. The father was calmly thinking to himself but the boy was filled with fear. The darkness was devouring him. He hardly "dared to take a deep breath for then you

got the darkness inside you and that was dangerous." The boy moves close to his father and tells
him that the darkness is horrible. The father
replies:

'No, my boy, it's not horrible,' he said, taking me by
the hand.
'Yes, Father, it is.'
'No, my child, you mustn't think that. Not when we
know there is a God.'
I felt so lonely, forsaken. It was so strange that only
I was afraid, not Father, that we didn't think the
same. And strange that what he said didn't help me
and stop me from being afraid. Not even what he said
about God helped me. I thought he was too horrible. It
was horrible that he was everywhere here in the
darkness, down under the trees, in the telegraph poles
which rumbled—that must be he—everywhere. And
yet you could never see him.
We walked in silence, each with his own thoughts.
My heart contracted, as though the darkness had got
in and was beginning to squeeze it.
Then, as we were rounding a bend, we suddenly
heard a mighty roar behind us! We were awakened
out of our thoughts in alarm. Father pulled me down
onto the enbankment, down into the abyss, held me
there. Then the train tore past, a black train. All the
lights in the carriages were out, and it was going at
frantic speed. What sort of train was it? There wasn't
one due now! We gazed at it in terror. The fire blazed
in the huge engine as they shovelled in coal; sparks
whirled out into the night. It was terrible. The driver
stood there in the light of the fire, pale, motionless, his
features as though turned to stone. Father didn't recognize him, didn't know who he was. The man just
stared straight ahead, as though intent only on rush-

ing into the darkness, far into the darkness that had no end.

Beside myself with dread, I stood there panting, gazing after the furious vision. It was swallowed up by the night. Father took me up onto the line; we hurried home. He said, 'Strange, what train was that? And I didn't recognize the driver.' Then we walked on in silence.

But my whole body was shaking. It was for me, for my sake. I sensed what it meant: it was the anguish that was to come, the unknown, all that Father knew nothing about, that he wouldn't be able to protect me against. That was how this world, this life, would be for me; not like Father's where everything was secure and certain. It wasn't a real world, a real life. It just hurtled, blazing, into the darkness that had no end.[15]

A fourth path to Mystery leads through a deepened sense of the ambiguity of our moral activity. We choose a model of personhood for ourselves. We will be open, listening and dialoguing with integrity and truth. We will be loving, respecting the person of the other and looking to his well-being. Although this is the model we choose and we sincerely wish to enact it, our concrete lives reveal something different. In the actual affairs of life a new tendency seems to take over. We manipulate others to get our way. Far from open dialogue, subtle domination is the game we play and the helpful lie is never far away. Our stated goals of concern for others cannot stand up against our self-serving interests. St. Paul knew the experience: "The good I would, I do not; the evil I would not, that I do." This experience of internal war pushes us beyond ourselves. We become aware of the Mystery we dwell within and look to it for explanation and healing. The pervasive element of alienation in all our relationships carries us beyond those relationships into an awareness of Mystery.

Although we each walk our own path, the path we find ourselves on may not be of our own choosing. We may wish an ecstatic experience and get desolation, to soar into Mystery on the wings of great art and have to enter through the humiliation of our moral ambiguity. We do not pursue Mystery on its own terms. Many contemporary Catholics know this for they have found themselves on a path they never dreamed of traveling. Their entry into an existential awareness of Mystery has been neither graceful nor reassuring. Disenchantment never is.

Disenchantment is a traditional and well established path to the awareness of Mystery. Many primitive tribes construct situations of disenchantment to mark the entry into adulthood. The initiation rite for Hopi children is a good example. The rite centers around the *kachinas*, masked gods who visit the village. During the cultic initiation the *kachinas* tell the children secret stories, frighten them with ogre masks, and dance to entertain them. But the climax of the ceremony holds a surprise.

> The children are taken into a *kiva* (hut) to await a *kachina* dance—a now familiar event. They hear the

kachinas calling as they approach the kiva. They
witness the invitation extended from within the kiva
for the dancing gods to enter. But to the children's
amazement, the kachinas enter without masks, and for
the first time in their lives, the initiates discover that
the kachinas are actually members of their own village
impersonating the gods.[16]

This experience of disenchantment is the beginning of mature religious consciousness. During
the rite the children naively believe the masked
dancers are really Hopi gods. The symbols of the
Sacred (the masked dancers) are taken to be the
Sacred itself. The unmasking conclusion shatters
this childish faith and pushes the initiate into
adult life with a profound religious question.
Knowing what they now know—should the
kachinas (and other cultic objects) be left behind
with childhood or is there a way of bringing them
forward into adult life? The kachinas must be
appropriated in a new way. The thrust of this
understanding is that while the Sacred expresses
itself through particular symbols (the kachinas),
any simple identification of symbol and the Sacred is naive. The Sacred is infinitely more than
the masked dancers.

In the past fifteen years many Catholics have
reluctantly undergone an analogous initiation
rite. The path to Mystery, one not chosen but one
given, has been disenchantment. Linking contemporary Catholics with Hopi children is not meant
to be facetious. The patterns of religious awareness although individuated in startling, different

situations, cross cultural and age barriers. If, as
Calvin suggests, the mind incessantly manufac-
tures idols (the identification of the Sacred with a
finite object) disenchantment as a path to Mystery is always a possibility.

In the Catholic world of the immediate past
there was a tendency to merge the symbols of
sacrality with the Sacred itself. In the minds of
many the Church with its laws and rites were in-
fallible revelations of the will of God. Mystery
had completely handed itself over to Church
authority. In the process it ceased to be Mystery
and became rule. In the mid and late sixties both
theological and cultural forces combined to un-
mask this faulty understanding of Church. What
was revealed was a very human institution with
both altruistic and self-serving motives. The result among many Catholics was anger, bitterness,
and disenchantment.

The influence of this disenchantment is reflected in contemporary Catholic Christology and
ecclesiology. The strong insistence of liberal
Catholics on the humanity of both Jesus and the
Church is a telling sign that they have just recently discovered it. The humanity of Jesus is the
indisputable starting point for contemporary
thought on Christ. The Chalcedonian doctrine of
one divine person and two natures is reintepreted
to affirm Jesus as a human person. Once the total
humanity of Jesus has been safeguarded the mystery of divine presence is addressed. Any simple
proclamatory statements like, "Jesus is God" are

shied away from. In eccesiology the influence of disenchantment is even more striking. The starting point is a consistently held distinction between Kingdom and Church. The Kingdom is God's universal plan and purpose which he is bringing about in always mysterious ways. The Church may be the herald of the Kingdom or the anticipated presence of the Kingdom but no simple identification between Kingdom and Church is made. Mystery, the transcendent meaning of which Christians call God, remains Mystery. No finite reality, either the person of Jesus or the Church, lays exclusive claim to it.

At first the experience of disenchantment appears negative. It is resented and seen as destructive of personal convictions and purposes. What was thought to be the case has proved otherwise. This is not merely the pain of being wrong or the pain of loss (the sacred has receded) but the pain of being deceived. Life in its most important dimension, the relationship to God, had been guided by an understanding of Church that claimed too much. But, however painful the path of disenchantment, it is, in the last analysis, a positive and maturing experience. It is more an experience of discovery than loss. It is the retrieval of the true relationship between Mystery and finite human reality.

Disenchantment is an experience of Mystery reasserting itself. Whenever a person mistakenly equates Mystery with finite reality, he creates an idol. An idol is not a symbol of Mystery but the

pretension to be Mystery itself. It insinuates a
total revelation and creates the false consciousness that Mystery has dissolved into total avail-
ability. In the idolatrous situation Mystery does
not appear within finite reality but is identified
with some aspect of it. In this setting the process
of disenchantment is also a process of disengage-
ment, a double freeing. Mystery is freed from the
idol's exclusive hold and the idol is freed from its
false identity. Mystery is restored to its status as
genuine Mystery and finite reality, previously
idolatrous, now has the possibility of being
appropriated as a symbol, not the usurper of the
sacred but one of its mediators.

The experiences of contingency, dialogue,
communion, moral ambiguity and disenchantment
are a few of the paths which people travel to become aware of their relatedness to Mystery.
There are many others. Wordsworth, as so many
before and after him, found a relatedness to Mystery through nature. When he is oppressed by
"the fretful stir/unprofitable, and the fever of the
world his spirit has turned to this scene of/natu-
ral beauty and the presence that inhabits it." For
other poets, like Eliot, it is precisely in the "fretful stir" that a universal presence is found.[17]
Peter Berger details five "prototypical human
gestures" in which a person might become aware
of a relatedness to Mystery. The experiences of
order, play, hope, damnation, and humor hint at
a transcendent dimension. Michael Novak names
freedom, honesty, community, and courage as

experiences which open onto transcendent reality. Abraham Maslow talks of peak experiences and Ian Ramsey of cosmic disclosures when the flat world takes on depth. Victor Frankl thinks man's consciousness of being responsible reflects an unconscious relation to ultimate reality. To awaken to all it means to be human is to be aware of a relationship to a More, a Whole, an Encompassing, a Transcendent, an Ultimate, a Mystery. Many paths, one clearing.

Sensitivity to the dimension of Mystery entails more than just the fact of our relatedness. The relationship has certain qualities and tonalities. We sense an intimacy yet distance in our relationship to Mystery. Mystery is both within us and without, in our midst yet beyond us. In classical theological language it is both immanent and transcendent. The fact that it is always transcendent does not mean we have no relationship to it. The fact that it is always immanent does not mean it is no more than we are. We have a sense of participating in Mystery but not of controlling it, of calling it our own but in no way owning it.

Secondly, our awareness of Mystery is fleeting and unbidden. Barlach wrote of God that he "conceals himself behind everything, and in everything are narrow cracks through which he . . . shines and flashes . . . cracks so fine that we can never find them again if we only turn our heads."[18] Our awareness of Mystery is similar. It is sudden and intermittent and engenders in us a sense of response. In this matter we are not the pursuers. Mystery comes upon us unsolicited. We are invited to awareness. In so many areas of our lives we view ourselves as initiators. Here, we sense, we are not first.

Our relationship to Mystery is also ambiguous. Is that which we cannot escape from for us or against us? At times our relationship appears gracious. Mystery funds our powers, supports our hopes. At other times it seems to contradict all we are. Mystery alternately seems to encourage us to greatness and then convict us of meanness. One moment it is a tale told by an idiot, the next salvation history.

There are other qualities inherent in our awareness of Mystery. Despite the fact that our awareness is mediated and often fleeting, the reality of the dimension of Mystery is beyond doubt. It is the "most real thing" we encounter. Despite the fact that Mystery seems to send mixed messages, our relationship to it is of utmost importance. Mystery is the ultimate context of all human activity. All reality, in some way, reflects its presence. If Mystery is absurd, then all our proximate meanings are the camouflages of death. If Mystery is not the source of healing, then our partial reconciliations are only momentary truces. Mystery, because of its pervasiveness and ultimate character, either grounds or undermines our deepest hopes and loves. Its importance is beyond measure.

Suddenly we are. We find ourselves in interaction with ourselves, our family and friends,

society and institutions, and the universe. In our
interaction with these environments we become
aware of a dimension of Mystery which transcends yet suffuses every experience. This awareness is sacramental, almost any finite experience
can precipitate it. When we reach our limits,
when we deeply dialogue, when our ordered
worlds collapse, when we cannot enact our moral
ideals, when we are disenchanted, we often
enter into the awareness of Mystery. We are
inescapably related to this Mystery which is
immanent and transcendent, which issues invitations we must respond to, which is ambiguous
about its intentions, and which is real and important beyond all else. Our dwelling within Mystery
is both menacing and promising, a relationship of
exceeding darkness and undeserved light. In this
situation and with this awareness we do a distinctively human thing. We gather together and
tell stories of God to calm our terror and hold
our hope on high.

CHAPTER TWO
World-Making

God is the anchor-symbol for a whole way of life and worldview.[1]

—Gordon Kaufman

ALAN WATTS once remarked that the most profound questions are reflected in ordinary language and asked in everyday conversation. "Who do you think you are? Who started this? Are we going to make it? . . . Where the hell do you think you're going? . . . Is it serious?"[2] Another of these ordinary phrases which reaches beyond its surface usage is, "Why can't you leave things alone?"

The fact is we cannot leave anything alone. Everything we encounter is quickly and compulsively interpreted. We do not long abide experience in a fragmented, chaotic form. No sooner has "the incessant shower of innumerable atoms," as Virginia Woolf put it, bombarded us than we are ordering and valuing, choosing and arranging. Shaping experience into meaningful patterns is the unceasing activity of the symbol-making animal. When our experiences do not easily yield meaning, we will "wring" it out of them or "bestow" it upon them. What will not be tolerated are unappropriated happenings. We will own, at all costs, what we undergo. This human need for meaning is cleverly satirized in Kurt Vonnegut's *Cat's Cradle*. God has just created Adam. "Man blinked. 'What is the *purpose* of all this?' he asked politely. 'Everything must have a purpose?' asked God. 'Certainly,' said man. 'Then I leave it to you to think of one for all this,' said God. And he went away."

To stress the compulsiveness of this drive for meaning is not to suggest that the human imagination imposes arbitrary patterns on the reality it encounters. The meaning that arises out of human experience follows the dialogic dynamic of the self's interaction with its environments. On the one hand, human symbolic activity is not so dominant that it is subjectivistic. We do not project patterns on reality from totally interior needs. We discover patterns, or better, patterns are revealed to us in what we encounter. Meaning is not solely the product of mental imagining but the outcome of the interaction of person and environment. On the other hand, we do not passively receive impulses from our environments and record them. The human person is not a Xerox machine, copying perfectly the impinging outer world. In engaging our environments, and through them the dimension of transcendent Mystery, we are actively selecting and pairing, disjointing and bonding in such a way that the neutral landscape becomes a personally shaped world. Meaning results neither from heedless imposition nor mindless accuracy but from the dialogic interplay of the person and what is encountered.

When we focus on our relationship to the immanent-transcendent Mystery, this meaning-making activity takes on a sacral character. We look for a way to acknowledge the intimate Whole which contextualizes and permeates every endeavor and is the source of our values. Our relatedness to Mystery generates a quest for meaning which functions in an ultimate way—not in the sense of distant and ineffectual but in the sense of "innermost" and foundational. Proximate meanings, no matter how hard won, cannot stand completely on their own. They must participate, if they are to remain vital, in an ultimate framework of meaning capable of sustaining them. When ultimate meaning systems are shaken, the activities and attitudes dependent on them quake. What meaning we assign to our relationship to Mystery or, more accurately, what meaning is given to us resonates in every corner of the human universe. Ultimate meaning is not just another facet of the human condition but the difference between a life of faith or fear, freedom or slavery, hope or despair.

One might think that faced with impenetrable Mystery, humankind would be more modest. When confronted with what is obviously transcendent to every capacity of the human psyche the drive for meaning might subside. From an anthropological viewpoint Clifford Geertz has noted just the opposite. It is at the limits of human powers that the quest for meaning becomes most acute. When we cannot explain the events which engulf us, when we cannot endure the suffering which overwhelms us, when we cannot bear the evil which defeats us, we do not become submissive but highly imaginative. We formulate symbols which account for and even celebrate the darkness and ambiguity. "The effort is not to deny the undeniable—that there are unexplained events, that life hurts, or that rain falls upon the just—but to deny that there are inexplicable events, that life is unendurable, and that justice is a mirage."[3] The instinct to meaning will not be denied.

Even death, the most opaque of human events and our most fear-ridden contact with Mystery, does not silence us. In the face of the "meaningless" death of John Kennedy, Governor Connelly felt compelled to remark,

> that the President of the United States, as a result of this great tragedy, has been asked to do something in death that he couldn't do in life—and that is to so shock and so stun the nation, the people and the world of what's happening to us—of the cancerous growth that's been permitted to expand and enlarge itself upon the community and the society in which we live that breeds the hatred, the bigotry, the intolerance and indifference, the lawlessness that is, I think, an outward manifestation of what occurred here in Dallas. . . . I'm not the least fearful of any foreign enemy so long as we have within ourselves not hate but human understanding, not passion and prejudice but reason and tolerance and not ignorance but knowledge and the willingness to use that knowledge. This is the only answer I can give . . . why he's gone and I'm not.[4]

From another tradition, Teilhard de Chardin in a beautiful passage suffuses the diminishment of death with meaning.

> God must, in some way or other, make room for Himself, hollowing us out and emptying us, if He is finally to penetrate into us. And in order to assimilate us in Him, He must break the molecules of our being so as to re-cast and re-model us. The function of death is to provide the necessary entrance into our inmost selves. It will make us undergo the required dissociation. It will put us into the state organically needed if the divine fire is to descend upon us. And in that way its fatal power to decompose and dissolve will be harnessed to the most sublime operations of life. What was by nature empty and void, a return to plurity, can, in each human existence, become plenitude and unity in God.[5]

It seems that there is no darkness which humankind will not try to light, or at least make warm.

It is often said that on the question of ultimate meaning contemporary culture has developed a capacity for silence. It exhibits "a negative capability, a firm disinclination to transfigure or to try to subdue or resolve what is recalcitrantly indeterminate and ambiguous in the human scene."[6] The need for ultimate meaning has been successfully checked. No attempt is made to symbolize the relatedness to Mystery. The contemporary person is admirably restrained, no longer fumbling for ultimate meaning but staring straight at Mystery without the inclination to cross over into it.

This capability, if indeed it is a characteristic of contemporary culture and, more pertinently, if indeed it can be sustained, is a reaction to over-arching metaphysical systems. Ultimate meaning systems have the tendency to pre-empt the possibilities of experiences, to fit randomness too quickly into patterns, and to synthesize the differences too neatly. In short, they claim too much. In this situation a return to listening, a posture receptive to the myriad impulses of reality, is adoped. This stance does not automatically reject an ultimate framework but is a procedure to recover anew the bond between the human person and Mystery. It is a search for meaning which reverences the richness of experience, a meaning which is not driven by what Charles Davis calls the "lust for certitude."[7] This appreciation of negative capability (which is different from its strict adherents) envisions it as the creative moment between old and new meanings. It resembles the phenomenological bracket which wants to "hold interpretation" so that "things" can appear in fresh ways. Our relatedness to Mystery means the question of ultimate meaning, although it can be momentarily suspended, is finally inescapable.

This search for an ultimate framework of meaning is motivated by more than a passion for neatness. The meaning that is sought is not a latticework of logic where all things find a place and appropriate reasons accompany every moment of experience. Ultimate meaning is not so much absolute explanation as a perspective which enables us to orient ourselves within the "givens" of any situation. It is not an attempt to cognitively capture the real but to relate to it authentically. In the meaning-making efforts of Connelly and Teilhard death is neither dismissed nor softened nor explained but told in such a way that we can relate to it creatively and not succumb to panic and chaos. It is from our experiences of being buffeted—alternatively threatened and reassured, exhilarated and anxious—that we seek to anchor ourselves within life. The drive for ultimate meaning is for the purposes of salvation not curiosity. This redemptive function of meaning is cryptically conveyed in Isaak Dinesen's remark, "any sorrow can be borne if a story can be told about it."

As our relatedness to Mystery makes us meaning seeking people, our need for ultimate meaning generates mythic activity. Whenever the word "myth" is used, some immediate ground clearing is necessary. Myth is a word cluttered with meanings. There seem to be as many definitions as there are philosophers, anthropologists, and historians of religion. Like most words that dominate theological circles (e.g., eschatology, hermeneutics) the more important the term becomes, the less precise it becomes. Our approach will be to bypass the problem of classification (distinguishing myth, legend, folktale, etc.) and concentrate on myth-making as an enduring function of the human psyche. For however im-

portant the form and content of any myth or set
of myths may be, the amazing fact is that from
age to age and culture to culture humankind
"throws up" myths as a natural part of its activity. The role of mythic activity in the human enterprise is what must be explored.

When myth is approached as a discernible
cultural product rather than a human process,
the widespread misunderstanding that contemporary humankind has outgrown myths is usually
the result. Myths, it is said, are the ancient
stories of the gods, the product of primitive men-
talities. They were helpful, even necessary, at a
certain stage of human development. However,
that stage has passed. We have entered into the
age of scientific thinking which has superceded
and rendered obsolete the mythic approach. But
the entrance of science has not meant the exit of
myth. Rather the rise of science has brought
about a differentiated understanding of our inherited myths and supplied the "raw data" for
new myths. The inherited myths, in Tillich's
phrase, have been broken. The scientific and his-
toric claims implicit in many myths (Creation,
Adam, etc.) have been discounted. This is not a
debunking procedure (although it has often been
construed as one) but a breaking which demon-
strates that the meaning and truth of the mythic
story is not equivalent to its scientific and historical accuracy. In fact, according to Paul Ricoeur,
only when myths are freed of the burden of being
science and history will their power to illumine

the bond between person and Being be recovered. Science has not displaced myth but performed the inestimable service of clarifying its role within human consciousness. Science, while claiming its own territory, has also demarcated the terrain of myth.

More important and more complicated than the differentiation of inherited myths is the fact that the scientific imagination has generated new myths. What is important is that these myths determine the values, attitudes, and outlooks of countless people. What is complicated is that their status as myths is often not recognized and so, as Gilkey says, they have an "under the table" quality which leads to distortion and contradiction.[8] Stephen Toulmin has charted the development of some contemporary scientific myths. He argues that many myths have "leapt out" of their scientific base to do service as total visions of reality. Evolution, dialectical materialism, and the second law of thermodynamics are legitimate theories in biology, economics, and physics. But when their role in human consciousness escalates, when they are lifted from their limited and proper environment and made the ultimate and pervasive framework of all things, the myths of Evolution, Dialectical Materialism, and the Running Down Universe emerge. The myths which guide a culture happen more than they are invented but the way of the happening is a process of inflation.

When a limited insight of a special field is making a bid for the mythic dimension of consciousness, one tipoff is that it begins to grapple with the mystery of evil. So transactional analysis does not remain a way of diagnosing human interaction but the key to a better world. Operant conditioning is not satisfied with the modest success of limited behavioral change but envisions the elimination of evil. This process of escalation often goes unnoticed or, if noticed, not thoroughly appropriated. The ironical result is that contemporary myths, even though scientifically based, are in the same unenviable position of inherited myths of a hundred years ago. They are claiming the precision and prestige of science when the fact is they left the field of empirical verification long ago for a more ambitious role in the human adventure. Although they do not have the "look and feel" of ancient myths and although their status as myths is often disguised as science, myths are present and influential in contemporary culture.

Even if contemporary society, as every society previous to it, is convicted of myth-making, the differences between modern and ancient myths appear overwhelming. The considerable divergencies in content (in general ancient myths stress beginning-time and modern myths either stress end-time or limit themselves to anthropological concerns) are outstripped by the stark disjunction in form. Ancient myths are stories of the gods: modern myths often take the form of an escalated idea which claims to have seized the heart of reality. Yet both qualify as myths because they function mythically in the lives of their adherents. They fill the mythic "space" which is endemic to the human personality.

Two contemporary descriptions of myth clarify this function within human consciousness. The first is from George Whalley:

> (Myth) embodies in an articulated structure of symbol or narrative a vision of reality. It is a condensed account of man's Being and attempts to represent reality with structural fidelity, to indicate at a single stroke the salient and fundamental relations which for a man constitute reality. . . . Myth is an indispensable principle of unity in individual lives and in the life of society.[9]

The second is from R. M. MacIver:

> By myths we mean the value-impregnated beliefs and notions that men hold, that they live by or live for. Every society is held together by a myth system, a complex of dominating thought forms that determines and sustains all its activities. All social relations, the very texture of human society, are myth-born and myth sustained.[10]

Although it seems that Whalley would lean to a story form of myth and MacIver toward an escalated idea form, both are aware of the common mythic task. Human myth-making does not create the given structures of existence but a world constructed on those foundations. It establishes the inner meaning and ultimate values of life situations and so becomes a guide for behavior. Myth is that story or formulation which establishes the world within which we live and out of which we act. In P. L. Travers' instructive analogy—we live in myth "as an egg yolk in its albumen."

Mythic activity creates world by structuring consciousness, encouraging attitudes, and suggesting behaviors. In the first moment the mythic story configures experience so that certain elements are highlighted. It calls attention to certain patterns present in the encountered reality and entices the person to relate to that reality through those patterns. Stories are told in concrete, individualistic terms and insights are tightly linked to singular events. But if the story or insight is to function mythically, it must transcend its singularity and display a pattern which has the capacity of gathering and organizing the formless but powerful impulses of a given situation. If a story or insight is to create world, it must introduce order into randomness and cast its shadow well beyond the temporal and spacial confines of its originating experience. Therefore the ultimate home of myths are the primordial situations of human existence. Trivial occurrences are not the stuff of myth. Mythic activity arises out of and configures the experiences of birth and death, awe and reverence, psychic and political struggles, the meaning of sex, the relationship with nature, the hope of an after-life, etc. The ambition of myth is not to be one more interesting but forgettable account but to become the structure of consciousness through which human situations will be appropriated.

Two examples might clarify this "attention directing" function of mythic activity. The Freudian rendition of the Oedipus story is a tale of the murderous conflict between a father and his sons over the wives-mothers. What makes this story mythic is that its plot is accepted as applicable to every family situation. It creates a world, a perspective, an angle of entry into the primordial situation of father, mother, and son. The epic of Gilgamesh is an ancient tale of a man struggling with the inevitability of death and the possibilities of immortality. The tale has survived and functions mythically not out of any great interest in Gilgamesh himself but because his story is in some way our story. The pattern of the story creates a context in which personal death and life lived in the face of death can be appropriated. And so a twentieth century psychoanalyst pondering the mystery of death can say, "The pilgrimage of my brother, Gilgamesh, helps me not to forget."[11] Stories and insights function mythically when they carry patterns which transform the stark structures of human existence into inhabitable worlds.

Mythic activity goes beyond, more accurately goes through, the shaping of consciousness to embody values and encourage attitudes. Myth is not a neutral assessment of the human condition but an attempt to actively engage the entire person in a particular rendition of the processes of life. In this sense it is unashamedly biased and asks from its adherents more than a nod of the head. Donald Evans has characterized religious (mythic) language as self-involving. To speak the myth is to adopt the attitudes the myth proposes. "In the biblical context, if I say 'God is my Creator' I acknowledge my status as God's obedient servant and possession, I acknowledge God's gift of existence, and I acknowledge God's self-commitment to me."[12] Even the evolutionary myth with its scientific facade of distance and non-involvement wants more than notional assent. This can be clearly seen when it is recast in the poetic language of Nikos Kazantzakis.

> Animals appeared—worms—making themselves at home in water and mud. 'We're just fine here,' they said. 'We have peace and security; we're not budging!'
> But the terrible Cry hammered itself pitilessly into their loins. 'Leave the mud, stand up, give birth to your betters!'
> 'We don't want to! We can't!'
> 'You can't, but I can. Stand up!'
> And lo! after thousands of eons, man emerged, trembling on his still unsolid legs.
> The human being is a centaur; his equine hoofs are planted in the ground, but his body from breast to head is worked on and tormented by the merciless Cry. He has been fighting, again for thousands of eons, to draw himself, like a sword, out of his animalistic scabbard. He is also fighting—this is his new struggle—to draw himself out of his human scabbard. Man calls in despair, 'Where can I go? I have reached the pinnacle, beyond is the abyss.' And the Cry answers, 'I am beyond. Stand up!' All things are

centaurs. If this were not the case, the world would rot
into inertness and sterility.[13]

This statement is not the proposal of a theory but
solicitation to a way of life, to stand up and go
beyond. Myths create worlds by providing patterns of interpretation and urging commitment to
the values they embody.

Out of a patterned interpretation of the human
condition and its engendering attitudes comes the
suggestion for a general type of behavior. Myth
provides a broad directionality, not a guide to the
complexities of concrete situations. To move
within the myth of the loving God suggests a
lifestyle of care; to move within the myth of the
liberating God suggests activity related to the
liberation of the oppressed. But the arena of
personal and social interaction is vastly complicated. To be dedicated to loving activity does not
assure the ability to love or the knowledge of
what "the loving thing" is in any situation. To be
committed to the causes of justice gives no
indication of what is just or how justice is to be
enacted. Myth paints activity in broad and
generally motivational strokes—to care rather
than to be apathetic, to be concerned about
others rather than to be preoccupied with self.
The working out of mythic demands in the
complexities of concrete life is a process of
ongoing evaluation and mediation.

World making, therefore, is an intensely personal activity which involves imagination, feeling,

and behavior. Although for the most part we are not conscious of our myth-making, we are continuously engaged in it. As our relatedness to Mystery is an inescapable given of human existence, so the mythic activity that springs from this relationship is inevitable. The question is not *if* we have myths but *what* are our myths. Whenever our biographies are deeply probed, a root metaphor appears, a myth which gives unity and meaning to our lives.

An excellent example of personal mythic activity is Sam Keen's story of the peach-seed monkey.[14] As a small boy Keen watched his father carve a monkey from a peach-seed. The boy asked for the "creation" but his father said that this one was for his mother but later he would carve one for him. Years passed and both father and son forgot the promise. Then one day in a conversation with his father Keen suddenly found himself saying, "In all that is important you have never failed me. With one exception, you kept the promises you made to me—you never carved me that peach-seed monkey." Not long after that conversation Keen received a peach-seed monkey in the mail. Not long after that his father died. "He died only at the end of his life." For Keen this story creates a world of promises made and kept: ". . . a peach-seed monkey has become a symbol of all the promises which were made to me and the energy and care which nourished and created me as a human being. . . . I discover a task for my future; being the recipient of promises, I become the maker of promises." The human person seizes upon certain key experiences, gives them mythic status, and lives in the world they establish.

Although Keen's story seems to be irretrievably his own, he claims it has universal extension. He sees his own history unfolding into the history of man. He becomes one with Adam, Oedipus, and Prometheus. "In the depth of each man's biography lies the story of all men." This is reminiscent of Willa Cather's remark: "There are only two or three human stoires, and they go on repeating themselves as fiercely as if they had never happened before." This fact of an underlying commonality to our diverse personal stories leads to an appreciation of the role of community in our mythic formation.

Myths and their corresponding worlds are, in the first instance, the property of communities. They precede any given individual and provide the imaginative atmospere in which we live. We develop in relationship to people who tell mythic stories and to some extent, because their lives are shaped by them, are living embodiments of the story. As we grow, we are in dialogue with the world creating tales of our people. These stories are encouraging and critiuing us, setting boundaries and modeling behavior. It is in the intricate interweaving of community myth and personal experience that identity is born.

One of the most eloquent examples of the interlacing of personal life and communal myth is

Elie Wiesel. His most recent work, *Messengers of God*, is a reworking of the traditional Old Testament stories in the light of his own experience and a reappropriation of his own experience in the light of the traditional stories. His telling of the Isaac story is a case in point. Isaac, like Wiesel himself, is a survivor of a holocaust. God ordered his slaughter then relented. Yet the name Isaac means laughter. The story of Isaac is a tale of the affirmation of life in the face of the despair and nihilism of holocaust. As Wiesel tells the story his own story is taken up and moved beyond madness and murder.

> Why was the most tragic of our ancestors named Isaac, a name which evokes and signifies laughter? Here is why. As the first survivor, he had to teach us, the future survivors of Jewish history, that it is possible to suffer and despair an entire lifetime and still not give up the art of laughter.
>
> Isaac, of course, never freed himself from the traumatizing scene that violated his youth; the holocaust had marked him and continued to haunt him forever. Yet he remained capable of laughter. And in spite of everything he did laugh.[15]

As in any genuine dialogue both the communal and personal stories are transformed in the mutual process of listening and speaking.

The central Christian mythic stories concern God. In Christianity no matter where you begin—with personal hope or societal obligation or natural resources—you eventually arrive at the question of God. Attempts to tell the Christian story without reference to God have always proved contradictory and reductionistic. In other words, Christian myths focus explicitly on the relational Mystery which contextualizes and permeates all there is. This does not mean that out of all the possible "objects" of storytelling, Mystery is selected. The meaning of the stories of God is not shown by pointing to a referent (Mystery) for the central character (God). Rather to focus on Mystery is to designate the ecology of the stories, the space where the storyteller stands. The stories of God originate and flourish in the relational flow between humankind and Mystery. The reality of God, although transcendent to this flow, appears within it and reconfigures it. The stories of God, therefore, are the faith appropriation of the transcendent meaning of our relationship to Mystery. In terms of theatre the stress on the relationship to Mystery does not propose the *dramatis personae* but sets a stage appropriate for the stories of God.

This conscious sighting and myth-making about our relationship to Mystery does not have immediate cultural resonance. Contemporary consciousness is much more at home in its proximate environments than in the ultimate dimension of those environments. Secular myths, following secular awareness, fashion stories which do not take explicit account of the relationship to Mystery. This neglect of Mystery is particularly ironic. For it is this dimension which penetrates and opens every environment and so creates the

need and possibility for the mythic renderings of
self, family, society, and universe which are
highly prized in contemporary culture. The dimension of Mystery which we encounter in
interaction with ourselves triggers identity myths.
The dimension of Mystery which we encounter in
interaction with family, society, and universe
trigger interpersonal, societal, and cosmological
myths. Flannery O'Connor once spoke about the
"engine" of a story. Mystery is the engine of
mythic activity and storytelling. Although Mystery is the source of mythic stories, why we tell
them at all, it is a source that often remains
hidden and unrecognized.

The result of this neglect is a narrowed
humanism. Amos Wilder has commented: "Contemporary man and his accounts of himself forfeit
the total perspectives of the biblical epic."
Biblical narration exhibits a holism.

> In biblical narration no significant dimensions are
> scanted. The private and the public are interrelated,
> the psychological and the social, the empirical and the
> metaphysical. And there is a robust reality-sense, a
> power in being, and it is related to the fact that man in
> Scripture, precisely in his total perspectives, is still
> linked with the archaic hidden roots and fibers of his
> prehistorical and biological inheritance.[16]

In relationship to scriptural stories contemporary
myths create a world with a small "w", a
truncated rendition of the total reality which the
human person encounters. Contemporary myths

are applicable to certain relationships within human existence but not to human existence as a whole. The world which is constructed is not a total context-world which attempts to tell the story of the pervasive and contextualizing Mystery. Susan Sontag has pegged this tendency as man's "increasing burden of subjectivity, at the expense of his sense of the reality of the world."[17] This burden of subjectivity produces stories which misrepresent more by omission than by commission. Any attempt at a wider humanism must tell the story of human person in relationship to Mystery explicity.

Langdon Gilkey has attempted to show how contemporary anthropocentric myths (myths which concern the self without reference to the dimension of Mystery) eventually arrive at theocentric concerns (the self in relation to Mystery). The initial focus on human powers and possibilities leads to an appreciation of the larger, encompassing reality and the need to thematize that reality if human nature is to be more fully comprehended. For Gilkey, many contemporary understandings of man (scientific man, therapeutic man, economic man) have a common mythic core in the assumption of awareness and freedom. It is assumed that the greater our awareness of the factors contributing to a situation the greater our freedom to better that situation. Evil is located outside human knowledge and decision. Freedom is always freedom *from* evil and not freedom *for* evil. But in concrete situations human activity reveals a more ambivalent orientation.

> If man's actions, even or perhaps especially when he has gained great power through his knowledge, remain ambiguous in basic motivation and often tragic in their unintended consequences, then such action must be undertaken and understood in terms of a deeper framework if it is to be creative.[18]

When humankind attempts to deal with the ambiguity and distortedness which is so much a part of history, it "comes upon" deeper issues and a larger reality. A mythic story which deals with our relationship to the Mystery in which we find ourselves becomes the necessary context for creative living.

The problem of constriction, a too limited scope, does not only belong to anthropocentric myths. There is a way in which God myths become self-contained, acknowledging neither their origin within nor their impact on human life. The stories of God are about God—up there, over there, out there—and not humankind. As person myths can neglect God and so become impoverished, God myths can neglect person and so become unreal. As long as the stories of person and God remain exclusive accounts of separated entities, reality is inevitably split and all energies are spent on building bridges over gulfs that do not exist rather than exploring relationships which do exist. God myths, if they are to be fully appropriated, must include, as a constitutive part of the story, the human person. In Elie Wiesel's language: "When he opened his eyes, Adam did not ask God: 'Who are you?' He asked: 'Who am I?'"[19]

A view of the stories of God which sees them as interesting tales of the divine person not only overlooks the interpenetration of the dimension of Mystery throughout all reality but also neglects the intimate relationship between story and storyteller. It is an age-old truth—in the telling we ourselves are told. It could not be otherwise. There is a whimsical legend.

> . . . and God, angered by inaccurate reporting and editorial guesses about who he is and what he is about, hired the human person as a scribe and began to dictate his story. (It is well known that although God positively-fulminates in speech, he has neither the patience nor time to write.) So for forty days and forty nights God spoke and for forty days and forty nights the scribe scribed. Finally the last word having been spoken, the exhausted God sat down (the whole time of dictation he had paced). The scribe finished the last word and stood up with the outrage of someone who has been plagiarized, 'But this is my story!'

To say the stories of God are also tales of humankind is not to say they are only our personal and social stories projected skyward. What we say of God is not merely Christian code for talking of ourselves. Rather the reality of God so suffuses the reality of people that to talk of one is to implicate the other. Our interpenetration by Mystery is so total that the stories of God, no matter how they appear, are never legitimately told in the third person. In this realm observer status is open to us only as a distortion. Dorothy Emmet has reminded us that when we say the Lord is a Shepherd we do not mean the Lord himself is a shepherd but that our *relationship* to the Lord is something like that of a shepherd to his sheep. The stories of God are not solely about God or about us but about the terrifying distance and incredible closeness between us.

There is a peculiar Christian twist to this process of inclusive storytelling. Christians believe that God and humankind have met and mingled in Jesus of Nazareth. And so a shorthand way of talking about both God and the human person is to tell a story about Jesus. The stories of Jesus have a triple focus. They are about God and humankind filtered through Jesus. In philosophic and sacramental theology the mediatorship of Jesus Christ has been thoroughly explored. But it has not always been recognized that the Gospel portraits of Jesus can also be understood in terms of mediation.

There is a way in which the stories of Jesus are not about Jesus. It seems that during his lifetime Jesus resisted questions about his personal identity. He deflected them toward the central motif of his preaching—the Kingdom of God and radical demands it makes on human living. Therefore attempts to uncover what Jesus thought of himself must go the way of indirection. For example: if, as some exegetes contend, the context for the parable of the laborers in the vineyard is that Jesus was being attacked for his attitude toward tax gathers and sinners, it is startling that he responds by telling a story of how God acts. It is argued that this certainly reveals something about how Jesus conceived of his relationship to God. "There is a tremendous personal claim involved in the fact that Jesus answered an attack upon his conduct with a parable concerned with what God does!"[20] Although Jesus' response might betray his awareness of who he was, it is preeminently another example of how Jesus redirected questions to the God-person relationship.

It is often said that the early Church did not display the same hesitancy about Jesus as he himself did. The focus shifted from the God-person relationship to the identity and work of Jesus. In the codified terminology of this shift, the proclaimer became the one proclaimed and the witness to faith became the ground of faith. Although this is undoubtedly true, there is an alternate perspective on the relationship of Jesus and the early Church. This perspective is reflected in the conclusions of redaction criticism. The evangelist was not a neutral collector and arranger of Jesus material. He had points to make and Jesus was one of the ways he made them.To some extent the Jesus who emerges in each Gospel carries the theological agenda of the writer. Therefore it is necessary to talk about a Matthaen, Markan, Lukan, and Johannine Christ.

The evangelist tells the story of Jesus so that

God's present activity within the community is focused. The emphasis is on the present revelation and the story of Jesus is reconfigured to speak to that situation. So for the persecuted yet hopeful community of Mark, Jesus is the suffering Son of Man who will return on the clouds. For the community of Luke, who must learn to live in history, the apocalyptic portrait of Jesus is modified. Jesus becomes the exemplar of Christian life. The difference between Jesus and the believer is down-played. The same Spirit which animated Jesus animates the believer. Like the believer, Jesus prays and attends worship: like Jesus, the believer forgives his enemies (Stephen). In this perspective Christology does not investigate the psychic make-up of Jesus but uncovers how the story of Jesus symbolizes the historical relationship of God and his people.

Therefore the Christian stories of God create world by disclosing the foundational contours of the God-Humankind relationship. This disclosive nature of the stories is their symbolic power. A mythic story is not a tale that is looked at but one that is looked through. It is the way we enter into the depths of human experience and the transfiguration of those depths. When a mythic story loses that power to mediate the ultimate make-up of reality, it becomes an hierloom, part of the heritage of the community but not part of its living tradition.

In this sense the stories of God have a self-authenticating aspect. The final reason why a story is "believed in" is because it has grasped the person and mediated to him the power of the sacred. The person finds that in relating to reality through the story he is healed and renewed. This power of the symbolic story to effect what it tells is captured in a delightful Hassidic tale passed on by Martin Buber.

> My grandfather was paralyzed. Once he was asked to tell a story about his teacher and he told how the Holy Baal Shem Tov used to jump and dance when he was praying. My grandfather stood up while he was telling the story and the story carried him away so much that he had to jump and dance to show how the master had done it. From that moment, he was healed. This is how stories ought to be told.

In order for the stories to function symbolically and carry the person deeply into the relationship with Mystery there must be an element of surrender. The lame old man "gave himself" to the frenzy of the story and, in turn, the story gave its healing power to the old man.

The contemporary Christian has a particularly difficult time in handing himself over to the community's stories of God. These stories are recorded in writings the youngest of which is around 1880 years old. They reflect the creative imagination of another time and place. We were once certain that the more we knew about the Bible, the more it would speak to us. Now, overwhelmed by Biblical research, we are confronted with the possibility that the more we know about the Bible, the less it has to say. One thing is certain. If the Christian stories of God, whose basic shape is given in Scripture, are to create worlds and mediate the sacred, they must go through a process of interpretation.

The approach of understanding myth as the perennial world-making activity of Mystery-related beings merges well with a current emphasis in interpreting the texts of Christian Scripture. In the history of textual interpretation there have been many approaches to scriptural stories, many diverse ways of prosecuting them. In the recent past the most popular way, almost to the extent of being the exclusive way, has been the historical. Harald Weinrich comments on this preoccupation:

> Theology engages—and here I quote from a theological essay—in form criticism, redaction criticism, the history of traditions, the history of exegesis, church history, the history of theology, the history of popular devotion and the history of research: all to demonstrate the 'complete historicity of Christianity.'[21]

In this atmosphere the first and usually the only question is : Did this story really happen? Can the recognized scientific methods of historiography establish the facticity of the tale? Did God *really* create Eve from Adam's rib? Did God *really* part the Red Sea? If history cannot support a story, its truth is jeopardized.

Since the Christian symbols and stories are inextricably interwoven with historical events, the historical method is undoubtedly legitimate.

The stories of Scripture refer to history and so the methods of history must be employed to reconstruct the factual character of any event. Yet myth, even when based on history, is more than history. Historical inquiry can place the story in a context, show its limits vis-a-vis the present understanding of historical fact but it cannot validate or falsify it with regard to its nature as mythic. Kazantzakis' tale of St. Francis' response to the novice who wants a book hints at the fact that there is a truth and power to the story of the resurrection beyond the refinements of historical explanation.

> 'Listen, my child,' he said, 'each year at Easter I used to watch Christ's Resurrection. All the faithful would gather around His tomb and weep, weep inconsolably, beating on the ground to make it open. And behold! In the midst of our lamentations the tombstone crumbled to pieces and Christ sprang from the earth and ascended to heaven, smiling at us and waving a white banner. There was only one year I did not see Him resurrected. That year a theologian of consequence, a graduate of the University of Bologna, came to us. He mounted the pulpit in church and began to elucidate the Resurrection for hours on end. He explained and explained until our heads began to swim; and that year the tombstone did not crumble, and, I swear to you, no one saw the Resurrection.'[22]

This is not anti-intellectualism but the acknowledgment of the fact that rational and historical inquiry does not exhaust the mythic story.

Besides the question did it really happen, the historical approach raises a second question:

What did it mean for the people who first told the story? Since mythic stories originate in particular historical settings and belong to a particular people, the question of how *they* understood the story is unavoidable and a first clue to its full meaning. This approach can be broken down into what was the intention of the author and how did it function for the people who heard it. How does the story of apocalyptic intervention color the Gospel of Mark? What does Augustine understand by the story of original sin? What did the covenant story mean for Jeremiah? This form of historical inquiry is extremely valuable and is an initial exploration into the meaning of any story.

Another approach which can be distinguished but not separated from the preceding two asks the question: What picture of self, others, nature, history, and God does the story convey? This approach reenforces the emphasis on myth as world-making. To ask this question is to explore the mythic meaning of the story. Paul Ricoeur succinctly outlines this way of interpreting.

> We now can give a name to non-ostensive reference. It is the kind of world opened up by the depth-semantics of the text. This discovery has immense consequences concerning what is usually called the *sense* of the text.
>
> The sense of a text is not *behind* the text, but in front of it. It is not something hidden, but something disclosed. What has to be understood is not the initial situation of discourse, but what points toward a possible world, thanks to the non-ostensive reference of the text. Understanding has less than ever to do

with the author and his situation. It wants to grasp the
world-propositions opened by the reference of the
text. To understand a text is to follow its movement
from sense to reference; from what it says to what it
talks about.[23]

In other words, myth is not prosecuted by history
or science but by the quality of the world it
creates, the dangers that lurk within that world,
and the possibilities that world holds out.

A clue to the "in the front of the text" world is
to investigate the religious conflicts "behind the
text." What were the enduring religious situations which gave birth to this symbolic story?
This "behind the text" questioning is different
from the historical analysis described above. It
does not ask the intention of the author or how it
fits into the theological framework of the community. It pursues the primordial human experiences—birth, death, fate, love, fear, hope,
etc.—that ground religious stories. In this way
the biblical religious foundation "behind the text"
suggests the shape of the world "in front of the
text." This collaboration between Biblical and
contemporary *religious* situations, this consistent
focus on homo religious will be the approach that
will interpret the Christian stories of hope and
justice, trust and freedom, invitation and decision.

Through the process of interpretation the
contemporary person's relationship to the Christian symbolic stories changes (in the language of
Paul Ricoeur) from a primitive to a second

naiveté. For the pre-modern person there existed an immediacy of belief, a flush-tight relationship to religious symbols, a primitive naiveté. But the modern person, precisely because she is modern, is a critical creature. She is informed by philology, exegesis, history, and phenomenology of religion. Although each person may not be aware of these disciplines, they form the cultural matrix out of which she thinks and acts. Consequently she does not have an immediate and undifferentiated rapport with the symbolic stories. They do not instantaneously disclose for her the sacred and lead to the experience of God. For the modern person primitive naiveté has been irrevocably lost.

Yet the symbolic stories themselves have not been lost. The modern person is able to inhabit them in a second naiveté. The second naiveté is not achieved by the creation and maintenance of an isolated world but precisely in and through criticism. The story is critically assessed in such a way that its power is restored rather than destroyed. Yet even if this is done, it is not enough. A wager, a movement of the soul, must occur.

> I wager that I shall have a better understanding of man and of the bond between the being of man and the being of all beings if I follow the *indication* of symbolic thought. That wager then becomes the task of *verifying* my wager and saturating it, so to speak, with intelligibility. In return, the task transforms my wager: in betting on the significance of the symbolic world, I bet at the same time *that* my wager will be restored to

me in power of reflection, in the elements of coherent discourse.[24]

But the wager is not merely for the purposes of coherent discourse. It is for the purpose of experiencing the sacrality which the symbolic story mediates. The criticism loosens the bound power of the story, "unthickens" it,[25] permits the sacred to flow through the symbolic channels of the story. But in order for this to happen the person must be open, must overcome the resistance to loss of control, must give herself to the story. Whether it is a primitive or a second naiveté, it is still a naiveté, a surrender, a risk, a wager, a chance. The hoped-for gain is God.

The reason for interpreting the stories is to release the God who lives there. The community has treasured certain stories, proclaiming them to be formative of its life. Therefore an interpretation must be accountable to the basic intentionality of these stories. But a story is never told, it is always retold. Why Christians interpret their privileged stories of God is beautifully stated by John Knox.

> . . . it is clear that we must receive the story as story and then interpret it as best we can, in rational and empirical terms, knowing all the while that we shall not exhaust in our interpretation what the story says and only the story can say, but also knowing that without the effort at interpretation the story will say precisely nothing at all. For a story like this [Kenosis] can speak to us of matters beyond our understanding only if it has also spoken *to* our understanding—and, within the limits of our powers, been understood.

There are two conditions under which a significant symbol loses (or, perhaps better, is shown to have lost) its vitality and power. One of these is when our hearts no longer need it, when all we want to say or need to say (or to have said to us) can be said without it. The other is when our minds, failing to discern in it the coherency of truth, are forced to reject it. For our hearts cannot finally find true what our minds find false. If they could, we should be hopelessly divided and any firm grasp of reality would be impossible. What we mean by 'the heart' in this connection is not something alien or counter to the mind, but is the mind itself quickened and extended. The wisdom the heart has found, if it be wisdom and not fantasy, is the same wisdom the mind all the while has been feeling after, if haply it might find it. It is a wisdom which, far from bypassing the understanding, enters through the doors of it, fills and stretches the space of it, and only then breaks through and soars above it.[26]

We begin with an inescapable relatedness to Mystery which generates in us a need for ultimate meaning. This need is expressed in the mythic process which is an imaginative rendering of reality for the purpose of relating to it authentically. The mythic stories create a world which encourages certain attitudes and suggests certain behaviors. Myths are primarily the property of the community and the life of the individual is shaped in interaction with them. Christian mythic stories concern God. They focus on the relational flow between humankind and Mystery and so are revelatory of both person and God. The basic shapes of the Christian stories are found in ancient writings and so they need to be interpreted. Through interpretation a world is proposed and the stories mediate to us the redemptive power of God.

The Christian stories of God are enthralling, provocative, and, as all who have told or heard them know, dangerous. What they are not is "all of one piece." An ongoing and powerful experience of God generates many stories. A vibrant tradition tells its tales long into the night. Real poverty is having only one story to tell and the Christian tradition is anything but poor. It suffers from richness. The Christian stories, the best of them, are unafraid, telling the chaos of what is rather than the order of what should be. They are not what Stephen Crites calls "pseudo stories," theories clothed in narrative, moral principles in search of examples. The God who bargains with Abraham and Moses will not budge with Jonah. The God who is a small voice with Elijah is a whirlwind to Job. The loving Father of Jesus does not visit the death of his Son. In the Christian stories of God logic is the last passion.

Although each story has its own integrity, they are not idiosyncratic. Since they all belong to a single tradition, they can be gathered into "mega-stories," patterns which pick up and connect common themes. In this way `many stories become one. Of all the possible arrangements of the Christian tradition three patterns which seem fascinating tell stories of hope and justice, trust and freedom, and invitation and decision.

CHAPTER THREE
A Story of Hope and Justice

Then I saw a new heaven and a new earth; the first heaven and the first earth had disappeared now, and there was no longer any sea. I saw the holy city, and the new Jerusalem, coming down from God out of heaven, as beautiful as a bride all dressed for her husband. Then I heard a loud voice call from the throne, 'You see this city? Here God lives among men. He will make his home among them; they shall be his people, and he will be their God; his name is God-with-them. He will wipe away all tears from their eyes; there will be no more death, and no more mourning or sadness. The world of the past has gone.'

Then the One sitting on the throne spoke: 'Now I am making the whole of creation new' he said. 'Write this: that what I am saying is sure and will come true.' And then he said, 'It is already done. I am the Alpha and the Omega, the Beginning and the End. I will give water from the well of life free to anybody who is thirsty; it is the rightful inheritance of the one who proves victorious; and I will be his God and He a son to me. But the legacy for cowards, for those who break their word, or worship obscenities, for murderers and fornicators, and for fortune-tellers, idolaters or any other sort of liars, is the second death in the burning lake of sulphur.'

Revelation 21: 1-8

THIS IS A STORY of hope and justice. It imagines a time and place not like now, a time when what is broken will be whole, a place where people dwell in peace. It may seem a beautiful and idle dream but there is an underlying anger to it. It is told because the present is death and tears and, quite simply, death and tears are not acceptable. It is a tale of defiance which will not abide Orwell's prediction, "If you want a picture of the future, imagine a boot stamping on the human face—forever."[1] This story rises from an inner stubbornness, from the bold assurance that our redemptive relationship with Mystery will withstand the ravages of evil and our own betrayals. There are many elegant descriptions of faith but at times it is a grip that will not loosen, a neck that will not bend. This is the story of a God steadfast in justice and a people who will not give up.

Stories trigger stories. The ending of one inevitably signals the beginning of another. They cluster and interact like pilgrims on their way to Canterbury. In one sense each tale can stand on its own; in another sense they depend on each other. None are complete until all are told. Together they form a tradition, a heritage of narratives which explore (in our case) the many facets of the relationship of God and his people. The tale of a new heaven and a new earth has ancestor stories, progenitors which give it power and fullness. The stories of rescue and covenant, judgment and apocalypse, resurrection and parousia carry a common theme. There are many episodes in the complex story of hope and justice.

The story of rescue is summarized in the passage of Deuteronomy which von Rad calls the "historical Credo" of the people of Israel.

> My father was a wandering Aramaean. He went down into Egypt to find refuge there, few in numbers; but there he became a nation, great, mighty, and strong. The Egyptians ill-treated us, they gave us no peace and inflicted harsh slavery on us. But we called on Yahweh the God of our fathers. Yahweh heard our voice and saw our misery, our toil and our oppression; and Yahweh brought us out of Egypt with mighty hand and outstretched arm, with great terror, and with signs and wonders. He brought us here and gave us this land, a land where milk and honey flow.
>
> —Deut.: 26:6-10

Israel is a downtrodden people, trapped in a political and social oppression. They cry out to their God who hears them and, with might they themselves do not possess, delivers them from slavery. This story is a basic confessional summary of Israel's faith that God was active in their struggles.

On the basis of this saving act a covenant is established. The story of rescue unfolds into a story of pact—Yahweh will protect Israel and Israel will obey Yahweh. There are two diverse stresses in the stories of this covenant tradition. The earliest emphasis is embodied in the Sinai and Schechem pacts. Here Yahweh begins by a recital of what he has done for Israel. At Sinai it is a simple "I am Yahweh your God who brought you out of the land of Egypt, out of the house of bondage." At Scheckem the recounting is more elaborate. It traces Yahweh's providential care from the calling of Abraham to the handing over of the land. After Yahweh has detailed these mighty deeds, he lays down the one-sided terms of the treaty. Israel must hear and obey the commandments. If they are kept, blessings come:

> You will be blessed in the town and blessed in the country . . . The enemies that rise against you Yahweh will conquer for your sake . . . Yahweh will put you at the head and not at the tail; you will always be on top and never underneath . . .

If the commandments are broken, curses come:

> You will be accused in the town and in the country . . . Yahweh will have you defeated in front of your enemies . . . Betroth a wife, another man will have her; build a house, you will not live in it; plant a vineyard, you will not gather its first-fruits . . . The stranger will be at the head and you at the tail.

Near the end is a curse both Beckett and Ionesco would delight in.

> Your life will hang suspended before you, and you will be in terror night and day, and have no confidence in your life. In the morning you will say, 'How I wish it were evening!' And in the evening you will say, 'How I wish it were morning!'
>
> Deut. 28: passim.

In this treaty the formal entailments of the divine partner are not mentioned. In the international treaty arrangements of the day no suzerain ever bound himself to a vassal. Yahweh is left free and so nothing can count for or against his keeping of the covenant. On the other hand Israel is tightly bound and their success at keeping the pact is the difference between destruction and salvation.

The second empahsis of the covenant story reverses the first. Israel's obligations are not mentioned but Yahweh's commitment is stated in bold images. In the story of Noah, Yahweh places a bow in the clouds as a pledge that no matter how heinous humankind becomes he will never again destroy the earth. Through the prophet Nathan, Yahweh promises unconditional commitment to David. "But your house and your kingship shall be firmly fixed before me. Your throne shall be established forever." But the most dramatic portrayal of Yahweh's constancy is his oath to Abraham. Yahweh has promised Abraham that he will be the father of a great nation ("Look up and count the stars. Such will be your descendants.") and Abraham has believed. But still Abraham asks for assurance. Then in an event of mystery and terror Yahweh demands three animals be cut in half and placed facing each other. The stage is set for the oath of God. Abraham falls into a trance and "suddenly a smoking furnace and a flaming torch passed between the pieces of the animals." The exact meaning of the torch and furnace is unclear but the import of the story is beyond doubt. Yahweh is taking a solemn oath before Abraham. He is implicitly placing himself under his own curse. "May God do so to me (what has been done to the animals) and more, if I do not keep the covenant." This arrangement does not include Israel's fidelity or lack of it. It is Yahweh's unconditional promise, his irrevocable commitment to the future of Israel. And the solemnity and power of the pledge is a long way from "let your speech be yea-yea and nay-nay."

The distinctiveness yet complementarity of these two emphases permitted a very flexible interpretation of the covenant treaty. This elasticity was needed for Israel's life was not an obvious, uninterrupted flow of promise and fulfillment. Israel's faith placed Yahweh in history, alongside them, fighting their battles and bringing them victories. Yet in the chaotic flow of events "God's ways are not our ways" was the lesson Israel was continually learning. Battles were lost: the victories belonged to others. In Palestine, a corridor between the military powers of the ancient world, the Israelite faith that God was acting on their behalf was constantly threatened. Each time the empires to the North or the South became powerful and encroached on Israel it meant not only political subjugation but religious doubt. While the covenant itself seemed secure, how it was being worked out was always a question. The very next crisis tested it. History is a fierce crucible for faith.

The major challenge to covenant faith was the exile experience. In 587 the Babylonians conquered the Southern Kingdom and exiled the Jews from the land God had given them. Once again Israel is helpless and cries from a foreign land, "Why has Yahweh allowed this and where is his saving power?" The prophetic answer to these questions ingeniously combines both strands of the covenant story. The catastrophes which Israel has suffered are the direct result of their infidelity to the covenant treaty. They have broken the pact and the predicted curses have come to pass. Yahweh is indeed active but he acts through "Assyria, the rod of my anger." Israel may yearn for salvation but it is judgment they have received.

Yet the Israelites are never submissive, never resigned to their oppression and exile. They expect rescue and they expect it from the very God whose judgment they are suffering under. Yahweh will keep his promises. Can a mother forget the child of her womb? Did Yahweh not swear to Abraham?

> For the Lord our judge, the Lord our law-giver, the Lord our King—he himself will save us.
>
> Isa. 33:22

So when Cyrus, king of the Medes and Persians, conquered Babylon and returned Israel to Palestine, the meaning was clear.

> Thus says Yahweh to his anointed, to Cyrus whom he has taken by the right hand . . . 'It is for the sake of my servant Jacob, of Israel, my chosen one, that I have called you by your name, conferring a title though you do not know me. I am Yahweh, unrivalled: there is no other God besides me. Though you do not know me, I arm you that men may know from the rising to the setting of the sun that, apart from me, all is nothing.'
>
> Is. 45: 1, 4-6

Yahweh unrivalled chooses Assyria for judgment and Cyrus for salvation. The covenant faith is alive.

Yet faith in Yahweh as the Lord of the historical destiny of his people is as viable as the next turn of events. And for many Jews these turns appeared capricious, undirected by the promising God of Abraham, the delivering God of Exodus, and the bargaining God of Sinai. A return from Babylonian captivity to virtual independence for almost two centuries is followed by political subjugation, first at the hands of the Ptolemies and then the Seleucids. Independence established under Judas Maccabee and his brothers, is followed by the uncheckable power of Rome. Under Rome, Israel's humiliation became intolerable. Rome usurped the right to appoint the Jewish High Priest, the representative of the people before God and after 6 A.D. Jerusalem was ruled directly by a Roman Procurator. God's people, once again oppressed, cry to their rescuing God for help.

These discouraging events of the post-exilic period pushed Israel beyond prophetic announcements of God's activity. These announcements were often contradictory and in the final analysis foretold disaster.

> From I Kings to Jeremiah 28 the Old Testament reports again and again the almost unbearable situation that salvation and disaster are proclaimed simultaneously in the name of God; and in every one of these situations, without exception, it is the prophet of judg-

ment—never the prophet of salvation—who is con-
firmed.[2]

In this situation it became obvious that God's
promises to Israel would not be fulfilled within
the existing order. History seemed devoid of
God's help. But Yahweh would not abandon his
commitment to Israel. He will bring a violent end
to this violent time and inaugurate another epoch
when the righteous will "shine like the stars of
heaven." The hope has escalated. Yahweh is no
longer asked to bring political independence but
a new heaven and a new earth. The cry is not to
remove foreign oppressors but to banish Satan,
sorrow, death, and sin. The deep anger and
abasement of the oppression is countered by the
sweep and majesty of the Liberating Act.

The strenuous conflict which will bring about
the New Age will be the unaided work of
unrivalled Yahweh. It will be accomplished "by
no human hand" (Daniel 8:25). Cyrus will not be
needed. At this stage Israel will settle for no less
than apocalyptic intervention, direct world-shat-
tering and world-creating. This is the hope of a
world-weary people, too long oppressed, too long
denied, too long abandoned. Apocalypticism
belongs to those who live in a tumult of events
which brutalize their dignity and self-under-
standing. Rosemary Ruether states it sharply.

> The apocalyptic view is . . . one borne of social
> extremity and despair. . . . Apocalypticism is the
> social religion of oppressed people, not oppressed into
> unconsciousness, but conscious of their oppression

and without the power to alter their situation under the present circumstances.[3]

The God of apocalyptic intervention is the rescuing Yahweh more vehemently petitioned; and both are the Warrior God who routes the mighty in the dreams of the downtrodden.

So far the story of hope and justice has unraveled in terms of rescue and covenant, judgment and apocalypse. With the Christian experience the plot of this story is reconfigured. The disciples' experience of the continued yet transformed presence of Jesus after his death is immediately placed in an apocalyptic framework. The main metaphor for the experience of the Easter Lord becomes resurrection. The import is that the long awaited New Age has arrived. Its advent, however, was not as expected. The end did not befall all at the same time. A single man, Jesus, has preceded humankind into the New Age. He is the first born of the dead, the first fruits of the kingdom. His title is the Son of Man, the end-time figure of the Book of Daniel. His task is to judge the living and the dead and he will return, most probably soon, to carry it out. Mark puts this meaning of the resurrection into the mouth of the pre-Easter Jesus.

> The high priest put a second question to him. 'Are you the Christ,' he said, 'The Son of the Blessed One.' 'I am,' said Jesus, 'and you will see the Son of Man seated at the right hand of the Power and coming with the clouds of heaven.'
>
> Mk. 14: 62

Therefore the Christian does not live between exodus and end but between the first and second comings of Christ.

The tales of rescue and covenant, judgment and apocalypse, resurrection and parousia merge to tell a single story of God and human-kind, a story of hope and justice. This story belongs to those people who consult the Bible to uncover the deepest meanings of their lives. How are we to interpret this story? What is the shape of the world it creates? What attitudes does it encourage? What values does it insist upon? What activity does it propose? And most im-portantly—does it mediate to us the power of the Sacred so that our lives are redeemed by its telling?

To tell the story of hope and justice is to direct attention to the socio-political environment. In this story personal fulfillment and achievement are secondary concerns. The questions of iden-tity, relationship, and family are considered in the context of the needs for social justice and political independence. Yet although certain areas of life can be "sectioned out" and explored on their own, they seldom can be completely dis-engaged from the total human context. The exis-tential and political dimensions of people cannot be separated as if inner reality did not have extensions into social contracts and social con-tracts did not shape inner life. This inter-con-nectedness of the personal and the social is reflected in the story-telling process. Tales of the socio-political order not only link to other stories of that order but trigger accounts of the personal lives that are lead within that order and either reenforce or challenge it. There comes about—not by previous blueprint but by intuition—a fullness of stories, a rounded humanity urged by the unity of our actual lives.

Therefore the immediate arena of the story is the socio-political order and its themes of domination and justice. Yet never far away is the inwardness of the self and its terrible battle to care and act beyond its own skin. The foundational architecture of the story of hope and justice can house many meanings. What meaning is chosen will influence how one will relate to the socio-political environment. Varying interpretations create varying worlds. One interpretation takes the fact *that* God acted and *how* he acted as the clue to the story. This interpretation yields a world of waiting, an attitude of disvaluation, and the encouragement of extremest activity. A second interpretation understands the fact of intervention as a common cultural assumption of biblical times and moves beyond it to uncover the values and intentions of the God who sustains the story of hope and justice. This interpretation yields a world of justice, an attitude of valuation, and the encouragement of interdependent activity. Both these interpretations and the worlds they offer must be explored.

An Interventionist Interpretation

In an interventionist interpretation the distinction between the historical and mythical activity of God is central. The mythical activity of God occurs in sacred space and time, detached from the chaotic flow of history. This distance from history is imaged spacially by locating divine activity in heaven or in pre-historical lands (the Garden of Eden). In temporal images divine activity occurs before time begins, in time out of mind. The initial and separated divine events are archetypal, providing models for all that is to come. The vagaries of historical space and time are stripped of their terror when set within the recurring patterns established in sacred space and time. The task of cultic activity is to bring forward primordial time to ensure order, a predicable cyclic running of the human and natural universe. In this consciousness, divine activity is not here and now; but here and now is successfully managed by what happened in sacred space and time.

The distinctiveness of the Yahwistic story of hope and justice is that God has entered into history. At certain key moments God directly intervenes as a separate agent of activity to right wrongs and redirect the course of wayward history. This emphasis does not eliminate God's activity in the cycles of nature but so overshadows it that creation is viewed as a saving intervention analogous to the God's historical activity. This entry of God into history means more than that the stories of Yahwehistic religion have some historical content or that historical events have generated symbolic stories which have become paradigmatic for Christian religion. It means, in its strictest moment, that the accounts of God's saving intervention, those of the past and those expected to come, are observable events of history.

At times this form of God's historical activity is explicitly insisted on. The fundamentalistic approach with its emphasis on the literal inerrancy of the Bible puts miraculous intervention at the center of every argumentation. At other times it is implicit in the way the stories are used. Does not a statement like "The return of Christ does not come 'of itself', like the year 1965, but comes from himself, when and as God will according to his promise"[4] suggest a separate divine activity? Although this first interpretation recognizes a mediated intervention of God (e.g., through Assyria and Cyrus), this mediated form is not the controlling perspective. Also this interpretation recognizes the difficulties which historical inquiry has raised for its assertions. For a modern historical consciousness which claims to exhaustively explain events by an analysis of the finite factors within them there is little room for an intervening God. What the stories of rescue and covenant look like when prosecuted by the canons of historiography has been the subject of explanation and reexplanation. In general, historical inquiry has reduced divine intervention, ideally able to be seen by all, into a religious faith interpretation of the people of Israel. But no matter what the difficulties with understanding the past intervention of God literally, the key to this interpretation is a definitive future intervention. It is this future, always-impending moment which shapes consciousness and directs activity.

If the interventionist interpretation relinquishes the end of the world emphasis, it falls into a privatized eschatology. The judgment of the end-time has as its first target the oppressive socio-political conditions. If this pressure from the future dissolves, the sinfulness of the socio-political situation and its need for transformation is not focused on. The more immediate end point of death begins to dominate. awareness and with it comes a world of personal sinfulness and salvation. The apocalyptic story no longer seizes the imagination and fires it with the dream of reversal but becomes the backdrop for the struggles of the individual soul. Death and particular judgment become the feared and respected eschatological moments. The end-time merely ratifies these verdicts. So if this interpretation is to create a world of social awareness, it must insist that parousia delayed is not parousia denied. It must hold on to an absolute and irrevocable act of God which will judge and transform not only the individual but the alignment of the "ins" and "outs" of society.

The world which the interventionist interpretation of the story of hope and justice creates is preeminently a world of waiting. Everything hinges on the activity of another, the invading God. This divine activity is not an undergirding, providential care which informs and guides all cultural endeavors. The story precludes a universal divine presence in favor of redemptive intervention. The longed-for activity of God is a disruptive overturning of the prevailing social situation. The world of this story is basically godless, ruled by evil and sin. Salvation occurs in those breakthrough moments when God enters to rescue his people. When we live in the world of expectation created by this story, one question surfaces over and over again—how do we wait?

Many ways of waiting have been suggested. Some fill the waiting period with longing. We cry out, "how long, O Lord, how long?" and do not move. We wait in attentiveness, poised but passive. The helplessness is so profound that our only response is to seek aid from a strength greater than ours. Many have criticized this behavior as an abdication of responsibility. If the story promotes passivity, it is self-defeating. It may be a cry for justice but it encourages no action on behalf of justice. There is no human effort to alleviate the social and political conditions which human effort caused. But the ultimate critique of this style of waiting is the

same experience which drove Israel into pes-
simism and finally into apocalyptic hope. Too
many have cried from the depths of social and
political oppression for God to intervene. And no
God came.

A second style of waiting is to provoke the
reluctant God to act. This behavior goes beyond
attentive waiting. It initiates activity which will
radically change the socio-political conditions
and hopes God will intervene and finish what has
been begun. Although this forcing of God's hand
does not seem to be an option which has contemporary appeal, it is a strategy which at one
time the story inspired. This style of waiting at
least partially explains the suicidal opposition of
the Zealots to Rome.

> . . . it was not in their own strength that the Zealots
> trusted; their trust lay in the God who had so miracu-
> lously delivered their ancestors from slavery in Egypt.
> . . . It is, therefore, a necessary inference that Judas
> and Saddok, when they called upon their people to
> withstand the Roman demand, also believed that the
> kingdom of God was at hand.[5]

This style waits by engaging in presumptuous
activity.

A third style of waiting derived from the inter-
ventionary interpretation of the story of hope and
justice is to wait in action. God will intervene in
the future to bring about an order of justice and
peace. This will not just be a temporary reprieve
from evil but the permanent establishment of a
new heaven and a new earth which will include

all created reality. In the present we are called upon to anticipate this arrival of God by engaging in activity which imitates the life of the coming Kingdom. The hope for the coming invasion of God does not breed irresponsibility or presump-tion but pressures us into activity which Christ will recognize as his own when at last he comes.

Although this form of waiting does not stress the "when" of the coming Kingdom, definitive intervention as eventual and inevitable is the core of the vision. The interpretation does not intimate that human activity creates the Kingdom situation. It is not the result of superlative human effort, the last phase of technological planning and political participation. The kingdom will be established by God's future act. The hope for this future exerts a pressure on the present. Human-kind prepares for the coming of the Kingdom by anticipating it. One way the resurrection of Christ, the proleptic presence of the End-Time, shapes behavior is elaborated by Herbert McCabe.

> The resurrection of Christ means that death is not just a matter of destruction, the end of life, but can be a revolution; the beginning of a new and unpredictable life. All revolution means radical change in the structures within which we have our existence, all revolution produces a new kind of man; resurrection is the revolution through death, the radical change of those structures within which we exist at all . . . The new world only comes through the death of this world. Thus every revolution which deals with structures less ultimate than this is an image of, and a preparation

for, the resurrection of the dead. The Duban or Viet-
namese revolution is a type of the resurrection in the
sense that we speak of Old Testament events as types
of Christ.[6]

Therefore the present task is to strive for
approximations, signs, proleptic presences of the
future Kingdom.

It must be stressed that this anticipated presence of the Kingdom does not cause the future
coming. Rather the future coming instigates the
present approximation. In theological language
the Kingdom is the "ontological prius of ethics"
and not the other way around. It is the future,
final God-shaped state which masters every
present and calls it forward. Therefore phrases
like "building the Kingdom" are fundamental
misunderstandings. The Kingdom is not a reality
that is coming to be. If the Kingdom were in the
process of becoming, it would be the product of
human responses to the possibilities of the
present. But the Kingdom is an advent, an arrival
from the future of something not contained in the
present. Socio-political activity may be an image,
type, or preparation but not the cause of the
Kingdom. Therefore a future intervention of God
is the energy source of this interpretation.

As was seen above in McCabe's theology,
people who live within this interpretation of the
story often view society from the perspective of
revolution.

The good news is an eschatological proclamation, i.e.
it declares that that which was expected to happen at

the *schaton* or end has here and now began to take
effect through Jesus of Nazareth. In other words, the
gospel denies what is, in the face of the future which
is operative in the present. In this sense gospel and
revolution are analogous, for the latter is 'a transforming movement from *what is* to *what ought to be;* it
seeks to make an is out of an *ought.* A Christian is a
maker of revolution, not just a talker about it.'[7]

Both the coming and content of the Kingdom do
not suggest a gradualist or reformist stance. The
Kingdom's arrival will have the qualities of suddenness and turnabout and be preceded by a
time of tribulation. Also the future which is
portrayed has little to do with the actual possibilities of the present. In fact the story often
despairs of the present and images the future
only in terms of reversal. The story does not
analyze the present situation and its emerging
possibilities but projects a final, perfect future
against which the present is judged. What is
inevitably highlighted in this procedure is the
wretchedness of society, its Kingdomless condition. In a strict Christian telling of the story the
present cannot be completely negated. The arrival of the Son of Man means that the Kingdom
has already been inaugurated and so "something
of it" must survive and enter the New Eon. Yet
the theme of reversal is the strong, ineradicable
atmosphere of the interventionist interpretation.
Therefore socio-political activity which antici-
pates this Kingdom leans toward a revolutionary
character.

The emphasis on God's absolute future has the advantage of providing an ongoing critique. No existing socio-political arrangement can be seen as a final fulfillment when faced with the vision of the lion and the lamb, the child and the snake. Injustices, deviations from the ideal moral order, are immediately spotted. The Kingdom functions in human consciousness as an everlasting image of critical negativity on all human endeavor. It points to what is incomplete and undone. Therefore the Kingdom is always more than any one revolution or the sum of all revolutions. Yet the absolutizing tendency in humankind is never far away. The future which any group imagines slides into God's future, something built into the grain of history. Leszek Kolakowski has carefully warned against such a "kingdom revolution."

> The delusion of which I speak indeed is not an invention of our time. But it must be conceded that it is much less abhorrent to us in religious thinking than in the secular doctrines which assure us that we are in a position to move with a single leap from the abyss of hell to the pinnacle of heaven. *Such* a revolution will never come.[8]

Revolutionary activity may find a place within the interventionist interpretation of the story of hope and justice but it is not the end-place.

The world which the interventionist interpretation creates can be characterized as interim. It is a time between better times. Exodus was a time of Yahweh's love affair with Israel and at the end-time wine will flow from the hills and wheat will spring from rocks. But now Yahweh and Israel quarrel and wine and wheat are not abundant. In *illo tempore* Jesus, the Son of God, walked among men and the Kingdom of God was tangible in the lives of many. The lame walked, the blind saw, the deaf heard, the poor were given hope. Christ will come again and the blessings he brought the first time will be bestowed on all who hear his word. We live now between his first and second coming. In these understandings the past is idealized. It was not as alienated from God as is this present time. And the future turns utopian. There will be a perfect, yet differentiated, communion between God and humankind. Since the attitude toward the present ranges from unsatisfying to unbearable, it is never directly focused on. We live between something that happened and something that will happen. We live in a world of waiting.

This story stresses the spectacular. God's providential activity in the ordinary ongoing affairs of life is not denied but it is lost in the fanfare of miracle and transformation. Christ's presence in Word and Sacrament is certainly affirmed but the emphasis is not that they nourish the present but that they sharpen the taste for the future. They are pledges of something more, enticements to the time when the river of life will flow from the throne of God. This interpretation does not deal well with the "ongoingness" of history, with partial peaces, compromised truths,

and small justices. It hungers and thirsts for
permanent peace, absolute truth, and total
justice. While affirming the genuineness of these
Kingdom aspirations, the question becomes—can
anything less than Kingdom be celebrated?

Since the end-time is the focal centre of this
interpretation, a natural outgrowth is the concern for the overall course of history. From the
perspective of the end all the pieces will fit. Past
and present events which now appear random,
relative, and opaque will become meaningful in
the context of the whole. That history is finally
God's, provides the hope that the waste of
history, all that is lost and destroyed, will have
redemptive value. A theology of history speaks to
every sensitive conscience about the pervasive
presence of evil. It is the message not to despair
for the suffering of the present time will not only
not compare to the glory to come but also will be
seen as necessary for the glory. "Did you not
know that the Christ must suffer all these things
in order to enter into his glory." Also confidence
in an assured outcome engenders a flexibility and
resiliency. The only true status quo will be the
last one. All else must be revised in the light of
what will prove to be permanent. The self-
important claims of every society must yield
before the absolute future of God. Ultimate
attachment to any other future is to live outside
the world of the story. With this future hope
comes the promise of a final resolution and mean-

ing. In the light of this, our sufferings are borne on high and our commitment to God's future is reaffirmed.

Belief that the final scene of the historical drama has already been written (and written by the unswerving hand of God) is a reason for hope, a principle of critique, and a source of courage for radical activity. But it often has the side effects of minimizing human freedom and not strongly enough insisting that justice is not its own reward. When the ultimate end is assured, independent of the human activity which contributes to every penultimate end, the full burden and blessing of freedom is missed. When freedom is praised as providing signs and approximations of the end but declared impotent to either bring it about or forestall it, a deterministic aura pervades the story. History will not fail because finally it belongs to God and God will not permit it. This conviction can subtly depreciate the importance of human decision making. An attitude develops that humankind does not truly own its history but merely rents time from God.

Also in the interventionist interpretation justice is often pictured abstractly. It is a time of reward and punishment followed by an enduring harmony, the perfect moral order. But the Kingdom is not its own ambition. It is meant as a metaphor for the relational reality that is possible between God, self, neighbor, and universe. When it is pictured as a state or situation, it often encourages activity that yearns for an abstract perfection independent of the people involved. Activity in the name of the Kingdom can overlook the rights of individuals or sacrifice them to the possibility of a better future situation. The story of hope and justice must give full seriousness to human freedom and encourage concrete care for each individual.

An Intentional Interpretation

A second line of interpretation appropriates the story from a different perspective and so creates a fundamentally different world. This interpretation does not stress the fact of God's intervention in the past and the hope of his intervention in the future. Some recent scholarship has suggested that divine activity within history is not unique to Israel but a common element of all near-Eastern religions.[9] "The whole society, and not only the Yahwistic theology, assumes that you can talk with God and hear him and receive the knowledge of his will. What you learn about God in the Bible is not the first contact with deity, it is new information about a person whom you already know."[10] If all gods are accessible for conversation and planning and fight for their worshipers, the uniqueness of Yahweh cannot be that he rescues his people and makes pacts with them. The key to the story is not the fact of divine activity but the reason behind it, not *that* God acted in history but *why* he acted. The story of hope and justice is a tale of God's intentions, his unswerving fidelity to the purposes of his creation.

This perspective neutralizes the chronic historical questioning. The persistent inquiry is not "Did it really happen?" or "Can we expect a final intervention?" or the next logical step, "When can we expect the final intervention?" With this interpretation the focus is not on the "if" and "how" of divine activity but on the deepest meaning of the Mystery we find ourselves related to. The story of hope and justice is a tale of God's heart not his hands. Paradoxically, for our age, the stories of the intervening God do not reveal his *modus operandi* but the concerns which obsess him. And the stories that do not speak explicitly of God's activity are the ones that become clues to how he acts in human life. The story of hope and justice chronicles the values of the biblical God.

The story of hope and justice begins with Yahweh hearing the groaning of enslaved Israel and remembering his convenant with Abraham, Isaac, and Jacob. Out of this seeing and remembering the power of God flows and his values are disclosed. It was not because of Israel's merits that she was rescued. She was delivered precisely because she was oppressed and exploitation is abhorrent to God. Yahweh reminds her that this was his reason.

> You must not molest the stranger or oppress him, for you lived as strangers in the land of Egypt. You must not be harsh with the widow or with the orphan; if you are harsh with them, they will surely cry out to me, and be sure I shall hear their cry.
>
> Ex. 22: 22-23

The second reason for rescue goes beyond God's unalterable opposition to exploitation to a positive understanding of justice. Yahweh is faithful to his promises, loyal to the claims that communal living impose. He understands Abraham and his descendents as partners and so he is responsive to the demands this relationship entails. God's values are nonexploitation and fidelity.

The covenant relationship flows directly from this act of rescue and is built, like all good deals, on a common starvation. Both Israel and God hunger for a non-exploitative, just way of living. Ernst Block talks of two different hungers. The first desires things that already exist. This hunger quickly devolves into greed and envy and does not release human potential but fundamentally misdirects it. The second hunger desires what does not yet exist. This hunger, at its best, fills people with hope and focuses their energies on the possible futures which are enticing them. The commandments of the covenant are born out of the hunger for the possible, a more just world. They concern the mutual demands of God, self, and neighbor which are not isolated from one another but intimately bound together. Allegiance to the God of justice entails doing justice in the social and interpersonal life. In this atmosphere the covenant tension focuses on the question: will the recently oppressed become the oppressors, will those who have suffered injustice inflict injustice? For Israel there is no doubt they have been chosen by God yet "the whole of Deuteronomy is pervaded by the feeling of a great

anxiety lest Israel might possibly throw this claim
to the winds and forfeit her salvation."[11]

> Rove to and fro through the streets of Jerusalem
> look now, and learn,
> search her squares:
> if you can find a man,
> one who does right
> and seeks the truth . . .
>   Jeremiah 5:1

> . . . there is no fidelity, no tenderness,
> no knowledge of God in the country,
> only perjury and lies, slaughter, theft,
> adultery and violence, murder after murder.
>   Hosea 4:2

Two of the underlying reasons for the lack of
justice are the preoccupation with false gods and
the excessive reliance on cultic observance. The
false gods which the prophets railed against were
Baalim, the gods of the land. These gods guarded
the cycles of nature and insured the continuing
fertility of both people and land. Although the
rites of these gods included prostitution and
drunkenness, their main offense was that they
diverted Israel's attention from the demands of
social living. Caught up in the comfortable,
recurring patterns of nature, the always-
changing, strenuous demands of historical living
dropped from sight. Justice, mercy and faith-
fulness were no longer the foremost response to
god. Incense and ritualistic acts ("Men blow

kisses to calves." Hosea 13:2) obscured the covenant of social justice.

Not only a "running after" false gods but a false understanding of the true God strained the covenant relationship. It seems that Israel came to believe the covenant demands could be met by sacrifice. Cultic observance was enough to insure Yahweh's protection and the fulfillment of his promises. The celebration of the mighty acts of the past were the automatic guarantee of the arrival of mighty acts in the future. Genuine trust in the covenant had turned to complacency. It is at this perverted understanding that Isaiah strikes out:

> Hear the word of Yahweh
> 'What are your endless sacrifices to me?
> says Yahweh.
> 'I am sick of holocausts or rams
> and the fat of calves.
> The blood of bull and of goats revolts me.
> . . .
> Cease to do evil.
> Learn to do good,
> search for justice,
> help the oppressed,
> be just to the orphan,
> plead for the widow.
>   Isaiah 1:10,11,17

Both the worship of false gods and the exclusive cultic understanding of Yahweh deny the fundamental bonding of the covenant. The covenant was the declaration that God could not be worshipped apart from concrete social living and concrete social living could not be just and caring apart from worship of God. Yet the gods of nature can be fully adored while the widow and orphan cry and the smoke and song of the liturgies of the temple can praise God while oppression and injustice reign in the streets. The insistence of the interpenetration of religious belief and social living is the gift of the prophets to every age and the electricity which charges the story of hope and justice.

The prophetic insistence on justice does not stem from humanistic concerns. Righteousness is, as Heschel puts it, "God's stake" in history.[12] It is not just another virtue or one more obligation of government or one more plea of the heart or one more cry of conscience. It is the heart of God, the core of his being; and no one knows him who does not know justice.

> Thus says Yahweh,
> "Let the sage boast no more of his wisdom,
> nor the valiant of his valour,
> nor the rich man of his riches!
> But if anyone wants to boast, let him boast of this:
> of understanding and knowing me.
> For I am Yahweh, I rule with kindness,
> justice and integrity on earth;
> yes, these are what please me
> —it is Yahweh who speaks.
>   Jeremiah 9:23-24

The absoluteness and urgency of the claims of justice do not come from the solemnity of the law or from pronouncements from the sky. They are rooted in the earthiness of God. God is compassionate, suffering with and taking into himself the pain and oppression of every son and daughter. The claims of justice arise from within, from the zone of God in every living thing, from the overwhelming care of the Mystery for all that dwells within it. Justice is the very life of God in man, his redemptive involvement in our pain.

Fidelity is the secret name of justice. Justice is more than an absolute ethical ideal, a perfect leveling, a complete equality. To live justly is to dwell faithfully and responsibly within the complexities of personal and social life. As situations change and the claims of relational reality change, justice may entail mercy, kindness, compassion, and love. At one point in the stormy relationship of Saul and David, David has a chance to kill Saul who, at the moment, is hunting David in order to kill him. He does not do so and for this reason Saul says that David is more "righteous" than himself. David has taken the relationship seriously and been loyal to its intricacies which at this moment—Saul asleep in the cave and David standing over him—means mercy. The story of Cain and Abel also stresses the relational and merciful moments of justice. When God confronts Cain with his murderous deed, it is not because the law has been broken. He goes after Cain because "your brother's blood cries out to me from the ground." And although justice would seem to demand punishment, Cain is pardoned and protected. Justice is about the relations between God, self, and neighbor and often that means more than measure for measure. In the contrasting images of Heschel, the justice of God is not a blind virgin with scales but a mighty stream surging through reality and bringing life.

The many moments of the story and the many moods of God are unified by this concern for justice. God delivers the people of Israel in the name of justice; he forms a covenant with them for the purposes of justice; he judges them for their lack of justice. Within the framework of this intentional interpretation apocalyptic visions function as a literary device to secure this foundational meaning of the transcendent-immanent Mystery.

Apocalyptic visions are the products of a "thirst for totality."[13] One way they express this is by painting universal pictures. It is no longer the history of a particular group of people (Israel) but all peoples, the kingdoms of the world. This might be the most harrowing conclusion of the prophetic period. No one group (Jews, Christians, Muslims, etc.) or class (rich, proletariat, poor, etc.) can claim God, for God is the movement of justice among all groups and classes. The reality of God does not exclusively belong to a particular people precisely because it belongs to all peoples. Apocalypse is the leap beyond nationalism. God is shaking free of chauvinism, refusing to allow any group to own him and tame him and turn him into a household god. God, as the painful experience of most religions attests, is preeminently faithful to himself (Justice). The fidelity of God does not mean that any one people will be favored but that the offer of justice will never disappear from human reality. The apocalyptic stories suggest that what God has elected beyond all else is not one nation but the just living of all nations.

The fact that apocalyptic visions are tales of the end-time also reflects "the thirst for totality." They are not *directly* about the ongoing flow of events but about a final, permanent state of affairs. Within the framework of an intentional interpretation the time factor, so central to apocalyptic stories, is softened. End-time language does not refer primarily to a coming historical event, however near or far. It is rather the escalated and absolutized way the meaning of the Mystery is expressed. The temporal image of end-time functions in the same way as the spatial image of heaven. It is meant in the first moment to symbolize transcendence and in the second moment to communicate the values of Sacrality. The rise of apocalyptic language parallels the growing understanding of God. Apocalypse is the strident yet hopeful proclamation of God's absolute opposition to evil. Evil can find no lasting place within a Mystery which proclaims itself as righteousness. The heart of the Mystery is justice; and since it is this Mystery which is the source and destiny of all human endeavor, in-

justice which contradicts it will find no home.
The Mystery cannot abide so alien a presence. In
this interpretation Christian hope arises not from
a future act of God but from his present nature.

In the interventionist interpretation the resurrection twisted and intensified the story. In this
interpretation the best metaphor for how the
resurrection functions is expansion. One theological interpretation of the death and resurrection of Jesus filters it through the patterns of
exodus and covenant. God rescued Jesus from
death and brought him to new life. This saving
act simultaneously fulfilled the old covenant and
established a new one. Although the way to the
new is through the fulfillment of the old, the new
is often seen as discontinuous with the old. There
has been a break—then a new start. Our interpretation stresses the continuity of revelations.
The resurrection reflects the same divine drive
for justice that energized exodus, covenant, judgment, and apocalypse. What is new is the infinity
of this drive, the variety of its manifestations,
and the inventiveness of its intentions. The resurrection deepens and reaffirms, almost unimagin-
ably, the impulses of hope and justice.

For Jesus the reality of God was so close and
caring of each person that one could hand life
over to it without fear. The symbol for the
Mystery was Abba, the intimacy of a child with
his father, and the most authentic response was
trust. This trust was so powerful that even the
closed and threatening future would open before

it. The violent and seemingly meaningless death of Jesus questioned, if not discredited, this lived understanding of God. Can the last power of life be loving justice if this innocent man is crucified? Does not the broken body of Jesus reveal the true meaning of the Mystery—indifference? The crucifixion does not raise the question, "Is there life after death?" but "Are there bounds to the fidelity of God?" The last question in the mouth of that hanged man was the fidelity of God. "My God, my God! Why have you abandoned me?"

In this context the resurrection is a symbol of the justice of God. God has proved himself faithful to the claims of his relationship with Jesus and through Jesus to all his creation. But the way of God's fidelity, as always, broke all molds. It linked justice to immensity. The resurrection of Christ reveals the boundless novelty, infinite invention, and continuous surprise of the Mystery. It is not that the end has appeared prematurely in Jesus but that there is no end. The temptation to closure which the human imagination is comfortable with, the tendency to round things off is too quick. Death, that formidable and most certain of all ends, opens into new life. And new life is not just another stage, something expected, a predicable apocalyptic category. It is a metaphor for the breaking of all categories and the restructuring of the imagination. The story of the resurrection is most certainly a tale of what happened to Jesus but also it is the revelation of the unsearchable riches of the justice of God.

The paradox is that the mighty, far-flung transcendence of God is at the service of concrete situations of justice. The limitless energy of the Mystery is devoted to the persecuted and the oppressed. It is through the deserted One on the Cross that the Mystery discloses its fullness. The Infinite does not swallow the definite but cares for it. This is the deeper understanding of the immanence and transcendence of God. They are not merely philosophic modes of a neutral presence but the structure of his justice. The way God is faithful to the relational claims of his creation (immanent presence) is by taking them up into his transcendent love. The abundance of God does not disvalue the least which live within him but is the source of their enduring value. If the secret name of justice is fidelity, the secret name of fidelity is grace—all that is beyond prediction, control, and expectation.

In the Christian rendition the risen Lord is the main character in the apocalyptic events. The end-time is transformed into parousia, when the reality which made itself felt through the resurrection of Jesus will make itself felt through all creation. If the parousia story carries the ultimate intentionality of the Mystery, what is revealed is the unsurpassable care for all that is creative of life. Not only is the Mystery radically opposed to evil but it is radically solicitous of good. In this interpretation hope does not arise because we know the outcome but begins with the felt-understanding that our pain and joy are taken seriously and ends in the wonder of the rider on the White Horse, the seventh seal, and the angel whose trumpet wakes the souls of men. In the book of Daniel the apocalyptic events parallel historical occurrences. But in the Book of Revelation the images break loose from history. They lead a life not restrained by the particularities of existence or confined to the facts of history. In this context, apocalyptic language does not break open the present by contrasting it with an absolute future but by fanning before it multiple, unspecified futures. The story of the Parousia is a tale of indeterminacy and its images are the imagination breaking itself before the immensity of God and the possibilities of humankind.

To live in the world created by the intentional interpretation of the story of hope and justice is to be continually aware of the claims of individuals and groups. It is to be faithful to the struggles of the relational world and to create institutions which are responsive to its demands. What is incompatible with the story is to retreat into the automatic, the other-worldly, or the egocentric. The automatic clamps ironclad procedures on flesh and blood situations. The intricacies of just living are brushed past in the rush for an abstract ideal—the otherworldly runs. Escape has always been a perennial problem of religion. The proclamation of a more has been twisted to mean that everything now is less. The egocentric suffers from soul blindness. It cannot see or feel beyond its own skin and injustice does not horrify it. It does not believe that when one is oppressed, all are oppressed. The intentional interpretation creates a world of engagement. To tell the story is to struggle in the concrete world of justice and care.

The story places us in a world concerned with justice and urges compassion. This compassion is neither pity nor condescension. It does not imply an inequality, one group suffering and helpless and another group neither suffering nor helpless but "compassionate." On the contrary, compassion is rooted in the felt perception of solidarity. It is the attitude of people who understand that, despite all that separates us, the last truth is a common humanity within a common Mystery. Compassion is the way into the lives of others to understand their claims and shape our social and political institutions to respond to them. This sense of solidarity is grounded in the valuation of life. The story stresses justice because life, every life, is valuable. We do not struggle for a more just society for the sake of justice but as a way of valuing what we have received. Justice is the last analysis in an act of respect. To tell the story of hope and justice is to live in compassion, solidarity, and care.

To tell the story of hope and justice is to live in a world of inventive possibility. The resurrection symbolizes the breaking open of the present, a restructuring motivated by justice. In this interpretation, the possibilities of newness arise out of the interaction of the past and present in the light of a future. They do not arrive from an absolute future. What is needed to actualize these possibilities is activity that is heedful, that is cognizant of all the facts present in the situation and create in relating them. Although the demands of justice are absolute, the forms of justice vary. Because justice is basically a service to people it must be flexible to all the dimensions of the human. Just activity is care-ful activity, gathering and weighing all we are. This story carries a mission and a hope. The mission is to hear the claims of all peoples, respect those claims, and create institutions responsive to those claims. The hope is that closed futures have a way of opening, that the Mystery of novel and inventive impulses which surges through us will fire the imagination of justice and continue to call us beyond exploitation to fidelity.

In many quarters the stories of God have a bad reputation. They are thieves of the human, robbing us of dignity and ambition. The attributes of God, it is said, are the finest moments of the human person projected skyward. With God reversing Prometheus and stealing our fire we are left cold and alone. Our only response is to admire a god who possesses such fine qualities. But the story of hope and justice, however interpreted, is not a tale of human projection. It is the justice of God finding what reception it can, speaking from the strangest of mouths, calling out from the most unsuspecting of places. This is not a story of our miserly justice and paltry hope pinned to God but of God's enriched justice and undying hope pursuing us. This God is not a thief but the giver of gifts. The tale is worth telling and will always be told whenever Christians come together. It is a story of a God, boundless in justice, who will not go away and a people, holding in hope, who will not give up.

CHAPTER FOUR
A Story of Trust and Freedom

His state was divine
yet he did not cling
to his equality with God
but emptied himself
to assume the condition of a slave
and became as men are;
and being as all men are,
he was humbler yet,
even to accepting death,
death on a cross.
But God raised him high
and gave him the name
which is above all other names
so that all beings
in the heavens, on earth and in the underworld,
should bend the knee at the name of Jesus
and that every tongue should acclaim
Jesus Christ as Lord,
to the glory of God the Father.
Phil. 2:5-11

BEFORE THE SON OF GOD could descend from heaven and die on the cross, Jesus of Nazareth had to rise from the dead.

For Christian stories the resurrection, even if it is not explicitly mentioned, is always the energizing event. The experience of the risen Lord urged the disciples to appropriate anew the meaning of the pre-Easter Jesus. From the perspective of resurrection they reclaimed the days of his preaching and ministry. They remembered that

when they were with him, they were aware of
God working in their midst in a powerful way to
heal their lives. In fact wherever Jesus went, he
initiated people into the transforming presence of
God. The question which Jesus sidetracked many
times became predominant. Who was this man
and what was the meaning of his presence among
us?

Jesus of Nazareth was the triggering center of
an event which restructured the God-self-
neighbor relationship. This event was not only
healing and transforming but mysterious and
overwhelming. It was too important not to symbolize and too rich to symbolize fully. In this
situation the disciples reached for titles and
stories which were available in the culture. They
hoped to unpack the meaning of what was happening to them and the meaning of the man who
made it happen. Although the only way to the
unknown is through the familiar, there is a
danger. Titles and stories are not the reality.
They only serve the reality. They are the way into
the Mystery revealed in Jesus Christ but they are
not the Mystery. This is reflected in the fact that
no one title or story is sufficient. Many are
pressed into the service of the revelation and all
are changed by the contact.

If the presence of Jesus stimulated the movement of God in human life, who was he? Some
have charted a progression in the titles attributed
to Jesus![1] This progression is more logical than
historical. Jesus is the servant of God. As the will

of the servant is perfectly attuned to the will of
the master, so the will of Jesus was perfectly
attuned to the will of the Father. But the relationship between Jesus and God was more than a
matter of synchronizing wills. Jesus is also the
Word of God. As the spoken word expresses and
reveals the interiority of a person, so Jesus
reveals the interiority of God. He is the communication of the true meaning of God. But Jesus
is preeminently the Son of God. The Son not only
reflects the will of the Father and expresses his
inner being but also embodies the very being and
love of the Father. So through the use of cultural
symbols the disciples' experience of Jesus was
communicated—to meet Jesus is to encounter God.

The full meaning of what happened in Jesus of
Nazareth includes his personal identity but also
goes beyond it. Although Jesus is the concrete
center of the Christ event, what is illuminated are
the general contours of the God-Humankind relationship. Jesus is not a solitary figure and his
individual biography is not the exhaustive focus
of Christian faith. The good news is not about
Jesus but about God and us through Jesus. In
other words Jesus is not a heavenly exemption,
but the revelation of the always and everywhere
interaction of God, self, and neighbor. To en-
compass this fuller meaning the life of Jesus is
placed within other stories of God. These stories
contextualize and surface the deepest meaning of
the Jesus story. In turn, the Jesus story specifies
and reconfigures the stories of God. What

emerges is a new story of God and humankind, one through which we can relate to the Mystery within which we live, and move, and have our being.

The usual combination of stories which attempts to uncover the meaning of the Mystery which was revealed in Jesus are: Creation, Fall, Incarnation, Crucifixion, Spirit, and Church. The popular rendering of these stories strings them together in a temporal framework. God created man; man sinned, fell from grace, and could not overcome this alienation by himself; God sent his son who became man and died on the cross for our sins. In doing this he redeemed us and gave us his Spirit who guides and protects the Church. In any chronological account the pride of place is the end. This story emphasizes the Church. The Church remembers the salvific events which, although they happened long ago, we still participate in through Word and Sacrament. Our allegiance to the Church, who is the guardian of these events and the arbiter of the moral behavior these events suggest, determines our salvation. Within this basic temporal telling many variations are possible and so multiple worlds are offered.

This sequential stringing together of the stories represents only one possibility. It has the advantage of being streamlined, unambiguous, and projecting the "aura of factuality" which Clifford Geertz says is essential in an effective religious system. Yet in this telling the full richness of all the symbolic components is not mined. What most often happens is that Creation, Incarnation, and Spirit act as presuppositions and connectors for the main moments of Fall, Crucifixion, and Church. Creation is the background scenery for the tragic deed of Adam; the Incarnation is what was necessary so that the redemption of the cross could take place; the Spirit had to be given before the Church could gather. When the story is shaped in this way, the resulting world is a place where redeemed sinners gather around the memory of their redemption.

Although any Christian story will give a powerful place to sin, a growing critique is that this symbol has become the controlling factor. The story concentrates on the quicksand which human feet are always in and theology elaborates endless and ingenious accounts of just how stuck we are. Our helplessness is complete and from this predicament we call to Christ our savior. The story minimizes humankind and maximizes God. From Sam Keen:

> I have a growing conviction that the Christian presence in Western civilization has perpetuated a disease in order to offer a cure. It has encouraged schizophrenia by insisting that man is a sinner (estranged from self, others, nature, and God) who can do nothing to save himself. Indeed, all attempts at self-help are indications of pride which only deepen sin. The word 'Pelagian' has been used to anathematize those who believe human freedom is potent. . . . The hard core of Christian tradition has always insisted

upon the impotence and bondage of the human will. It
has said loud and clear—'You can't. You can't heal
yourself. Your only hope is in accepting *the* physician
sent from God' (whose credentials are certified by the
church).

. . .

This we know about psychopathology—at the heart of
'illness' is the impotent child who is still crying, 'I
can't. You do it for me.' And it is clear that the
moment in therapy when the patient begins to 'get
well' is when he says, 'I am responsible for my
feelings, my actions, and my style of life. In spite of
parents, family, friends or the surrounding culture, I
alone can make the decision to outgrow my dis-ease
and to establish a way of life that is satisfying. There
is no magic. There is no automatic dispenser of grace.
There are no saviors. My final dignity is in my ability
to choose my style of life.'[2]

From Herbert Richardson:

A theology which makes redemption into its sole or
primary theme will be ambivalent about the fact of
redemption itself. It will have a 'vested interest' in
man's sin and weakness, for if these were ever fully
overcome, the presupposition of Christ's redeeming
work would be lost. Hence, theologies of redemption
tenaciously defend the sinfulness of man and view
with suspicion every secular therapy that attempts to
overcome or alleviate man's weakness. They are
politically and socially conservative, threatened by the
development of psychoanalysis, social work, and
political programs for the improvement of human life.
These therapies appear to make religion useless. They
cause a loss of vocational purpose in many clergymen,
who ask what they can do that the new scientific
techniques cannot do better. This is what the secular

theologians mean when they say that science and technology are pushing God out of the world: that secular therapies are destroying the anthropological presupposition of a religion whose conception of God is exclusively redemptive.[3]

The argument against this way of telling the story is not based on theological subtleties but on the type of world that is created. The story is not serving the health of the individual and the community. Its power, contrary to its intention, is not redemptive but oppressive.

An alternate way of relating the symbolic components of the story is to connect them in terms of an inner theological logic rather than by a temporal sequence. One theological rendition would be to link Creation, Incarnation, and Spirit into one set of meanings and Fall, Crucifixion, and Church into another. The result is not two different stories and therefore two different worlds but a story within a story and therefore a multi-dimensional world. This complex world might better reflect both the possibilities and entrapments of human life. It might also provide a way of relating to God not only through our need but also through our strength.

Creation, Incarnation, and Spirit

Israel's theology of creation is a secondary, bolstering dimension of her faith. Her primary concern and the focus through which everything else was appropriated was God's saving activity in history. In this context, creation is not considered in itself but as a prologue to saving history. Also by linking the concerns of the rescuing God to the power of the creating God Israel's salvation was assured. Not only does Yahweh have the intention to save Israel he has the might to carry it out. Second Isaiah states the connection well.

> Thus speaks the Lord who is God,
> he who created the skies and stretches them out,
> who fashioned the earth and all that grows in it,
> who gave breath to its people
> the breath of life to all who walk upon it.
> I, the Lord, have called you with righteous purpose
> and taken you by the hand;
> I have formed you, and appointed you
> to be a light to all peoples,
> a beacon for the nations,
> to open eyes that are blind,
> to bring captives out of prison,
> out of the dungeons where they lie in darkness.
> Is. 42:5-7

In Old Testament theology, God the Creator who called all things out of nothing functions as the foundation for the more impressive work of creating the people of Israel.

This narrow focus on the creation stories do them a disservice. Not only is God's relation to nature slighted but there is a tendency to keep him within the household of Israel and not allow him the universal role of maker of heaven and earth. But the stories on one level are a proclamation that Yahweh is not a tribal deity. He has created all and he cares for all. These contrasting emphases are reflected in the varying reasons for keeping the Sabbath. In Deuteronomy the justification arises out of Israel's exodus experience.

> You shall remember that you were a servant in the land of Egypt, and the Lord your God brought you out then with a mighty hand and an outstretched arm; therefore the Lord your God commanded you to keep the sabbath day.
> Deut. 5:15

On the other hand, in the Exodus decalogue the Sabbath is observed because "in six days Yahweh made the heavens and the earth and the sea and all that these held, but on the seventh day he rested; that is why Yahweh has blessed the Sabbath day and made it sacred." The first rationale makes the Sabbath a distinctively Jewish feast to be celebrated by no other people. The second understanding imposes the Sabbath on all creation. It is this second understanding of creation which begins our story.

The Book of Genesis contains two creation accounts, Gn. 1-2:4 (the Priestly tradition) and Gn. 2:5-25 (the Yahwist tradition). Although they differ greatly in style, they share a common view of man. Man is the pinacle of creation and the master of nature. All created things are meant to serve him. Yet despite this paramount similarity each account has its own theological orientation. The Priestly writer sets man within the rest of creation but also places man and the rest of creation within the context of Sabbath. The Yahwist emphasizes the character and role of man. If both these emphases are pursued, the story of creation, incarnation, and spirit begins to unfold.

The seven days of creation are not so much time-lags as value statements. They represent a hierarchical ordering, a positioning in terms of importance and purpose. All that is created from the first to the fifth day are for the purpose of that which was created on the sixth. And all that is created, from the first to the sixth day, is for the purpose of the seventh day—the presence of God. "It would be sheer folly to regard this resting of God's which concluded the Creation as something like a turning away from the world by God: it is in fact a particularly mysterious gracious turning towards his Creation."[4] God's personal presence to his creation confers holiness on it. The purpose of creation is to delight in this holiness. Creation has no purposes outside of itself. Its reason for existing is to enjoy itself and glorify God whose Sabbath presence permeates it with holiness.

Herbert Richardson attempts to understand the holiness which God's Sabbath presence communicates to all creation through the category of dignity.[5] Dignity is the basis of both tragedy and meaning. The tragic only happens to important people. If there is not a previous dignity, then the fall may be sad but it is not tragic. So it is argued that Macbeth is truly a tragic figure but Willy

Loman in *Death of a Salesman* is not. Macbeth was once a great and loyal king but Willy was always a third-rate salesman. In this context it is interesting to note Eric Auerbach's remark about the Gospel portrayal of Peter. Classical literature had difficulty in seeing ordinary people as the subjects of tragedy. Without dignity they did not qualify. But in the Gospels the ordinary man Peter is revealed in his greatness and weakness. He is the subject of the tragedy of friendship and denial. (Of course, for the believer, Peter's story ends a comedy: "You know all things, Lord: you know that I love you.") In the perspective of the Creation story all are capable of tragedy because all have a dignity granted by the presence of God.

Dignity is also the basis of meaning. No one can quite get through a book dealing with theological topics today without mentioning the problem of meaning (including the second chapter of this book). Meaning is often understood as the relating of our individual activity to a larger whole. Inserted into this larger context we have sense of who we are, our powers are engaged and we move forward. Yet even where meaning is present a deeper question appears. Is what I am doing valuable? Does it have worth? And more importantly, do I have worth? Meaningfulness is a crucial need of the human person but it does not of itself insure dignity; and without dignity the way we fit into it all does not seem to matter.

Since God has created the world for holiness

(for dignity, worth, and meaning) and all holiness comes from God, he must be personally present in order to effect the world's fulfillment. "The Sabbath is . . . the world's aptitude for the incarnation."[6] The story now moves from creation to incarnation and picks up a centuries-old debate between Thomists and Scotists. The question is: if Adam did not sin, would Christ have come? The question is not sheer speculation. It is meant to determine our response to the incarnation of the Son of God. If Christ came only because Adam sinned, our response is one of gratitude toward our Redeemer. But if Christ would have come even if Adam had not sinned, our response to him is to welcome a friend. He came because we were made for him and his presence makes us holy and we delight in ourselves and in him. He came primarily because he wanted to, not because we needed him. This is the reason of a friend whose presence brings dignity and worth. An old catechism holds that our reason for existing is to enjoy God forever. The incarnation is the declaration that God has the same idea.

Through the incarnation we are holy (dignified) because God is with us. With the sending of the spirit we are holy not because God is present *with* us but because God is present *in* us. Jesus Christ sent the Holy Spirit out of love. In becoming man the Son of God entered into friendship with us. The yearning of friendship always seems to reach beyond the possible. Gabriel Marcel says, "To love a being is to say: 'Thou, thou shalt not die'." For friendship to continue there must be communion. For this reason after the break point of death, Jesus Christ sends the Holy Spirit to dwell in us. Through the Holy Spirit we maintain communion with him. The Holy Spirit is the relational link between us and Christ. Richardson wants to conceptualize this reality by saying the Holy Spirit is one person dwelling in two persons (Christ and us). The Spirit is the confidence that "neither death nor life, no angel, no prince, nothing that exists, nothing still to come, not any power or height or depth nor any created thing can ever come between us and the love of God made visible in Christ Jesus our Lord" (Rm. 8:38-39).

Creation makes way for Incarnation and Incarnation unfolds into Spirit. All three symbols have a common aim. They wish the sanctification of the world through the presence and indwelling of God. This intimacy of God and humankind does not imply an identity or the divinization of human nature. God and the world are kept distinct as the difference between the sixth and seventh day suggests. But the seventh day is an opening into creation, a space for the Son. And the Son of God who is our friend and desires an undying communion with us bequeaths the Holy Spirit. God, our creator and friend, is now our Paraclete, the companion of our inmost selves who

. . . knows us not only better than even our closest
friends know us, but even better than we know ourselves. For when we do not know our true desires, the
Holy Spirit interprets them to God for us. When we do
not know the way to turn, the Spirit leads us. When
we are weighed down by doubts and despair, the
Spirit preserves our soul. When we cannot hold our
lives in our own hands, then we know they will be held
in the hand of God.[7]

Creation, Incarnation, and Spirit urge us to
dance in the glory of God and through that glory
to delight in the dignity of all created things.

In the world of this story, Christ plays in ten
thousand places and "we greet him the days we
meet him and bless when we understand."[8] It is a
world of sanctity and reverence where the relationship to Mystery means the unsurpassable
worth of all things. Dignity is God's gift to all he
loves. Creation, Incarnation, and Spirit is a tale
of friendship and enjoyment. It encourages us to
rest in each other and in God. It is the liberating
news that creation in the presence of God is its
own purpose and our truest song is one of praise.
Most important of all it convicts us of beauty and
tells us that is enough. This telling of the symbols
configures our relationship to Mystery into a
world of holiness and wonder.

The creation account of Gn. 2 focuses directly
on humankind. Man comes to be by an intimate
act of God. "Then he breathed into his nostrils a
breath of life, and thus man became a living

being." Von Rad sees an element of gloom in this view of man. "Life is possessed by man only in virtue of that breath; and this latter is in no sense inherently associated with his body, and any withholding of this ephemeral gift would throw man back to a state of dead matter."[9] But the opposite of the possibility of withholding is the fact of sustaining. God does not create and then step back and watch his creation move on its own. Each breath is the affirmation of the presence of God to human life. The breath of God is Kazantzakis's great wind blowing through every living thing.

Also in the story, humankind has kinship with, yet is master of, all created reality. Man is the dust of earth and so shares existence with all of creation. Yet it is he who has charge of the garden and who names the animals. It is this balance between kinship and lordship that has been at the center of ecological discussions. Kinship demands reverence; lordship demands that we use the universe to serve the human community.

The story describes the life of humankind in terms of interdependency, friendship, sexuality, and healthy community. The pronouncement of God that it is "not good that man should be alone" stresses the relational aspect of human existence. Any sustained movement away from human interacting cuts across the grain of created reality. Pride, the elevation of the self above human relating, and sloth, the failure to respond, are the classic ways we reverse God's intention. In the story, the woman is the help-mate, the friend of man. Sexual union between them is natural and expected for they both used to be one. The description of the origin of woman from the rib of man is not meant as a chauvinist reflection. Although it may reflect the thinking of a patriarchal society, its purpose is not to re-enforce male superiority. In fact, the argument that it is from the side of man and so symbolized an equality cannot be completely dismissed. The point of the segment is to explain and legitimize the sexual drive for union. Finally, the man and woman live with each other in nakedness and without shame. The goal of the interdependent sexuality and friendship is healthy community.

This whole account of what it is to be human—to be related to God, to be both kin and master of the earth, to live in interdependency, sexuality, friendship, and community—is pervaded by the sense of entrustment. Humankind is trusted by God with the Garden ("Yahweh took the man and settled him in the garden of Eden to cultivate and take care of it") and with each other ("This is why a man leaves his father and mother and joins himself to his wife, and they become one body."). This is preeminently the story of trusted crea-tures, empowered by God to live life and care for creation.

It is the contention of Walter Brueggemann that the Yahwist theologian who constructed the creation account of Gn. 2 looked at David and wrote of Adam. "The J account of Genesis 2, I suggest, is the David career now generalized as the way to be human."[10] The actions of David instigated a theological revolution. David lived and acted out of the belief that God was passionately committed to him. He was the trusted creature and this enabled him to act freely and creatively. Brueggemann traces the freedom of David to act in a new way through three incidents.

The first incident concerns David and Ahimelech, the priest of the shrine at Nob. David and his men are fleeing for their lives and arrive hungry at the shrine. The only bread available is consecrated. The priest wants to make sure the soldiers are ritually pure. David's response is not clear but the thrust seems to be that even though they are on a profane journey, a military campaign, they are pure because they have kept the ancient rules of battle and have not had intercourse with women for three days. This might mean that David had shifted the notion of the holy from shrine activity to warring or it might just be an expedient lie, for at the time he was not on a campaign but fleeing from Saul. But whatever the interpretation David has freely maneuvered the holy to suit his situation.

> Either way David is not bound by the normal notion of what is qodes [holy]. He subordinates that conventional notion to the problem at hand, namely his safe getaway. What remains is the primacy of his welfare

and that of his men. If *qodes* still functions as a
meaningful term, it now refers to the well-being of
his party on the way to royal power. Against the
narrower notions of holy which had been held, this is
a revolutionary affirmation made good by his readi-
ness to act upon it.[11]

The basis of David's boldness is his consciousness
of being the trusted creature.

A second incident concerns the death of the
illegitimate son of David and Bathsheba. While
the child is dying, David keeps a strict fast and
spends the night on the ground. His officials try
to get him to eat but he refuses. However when
David finds out the child has finally died, he rises
from the ground, bathes, anoints himself, and
eats. His officials now wonder why David is not
mourning. David answers:

> When the child was alive . . . I fasted and wept
> because I kept thinking, 'Who knows? Perhaps Yah-
> weh will take pity on me and the child will live.' But
> now he is dead, why should I fast? Can I bring him
> back again? I shall go to him but he cannot come back
> to me.
>
> 2 Sam. 12:22-23

Once again David moves against the conven-
tional taboos. He is unconcerned about the ritual
uncleanness of death and the fact that custom
dictates to mourn at death and refrain during
illness. For David faith is about life and about
what is possible within the limits of life. He is not
awed by the power of death and paralyzed with

fear before its presence. The child is dead: life must go on.

> David's reaction to the death of his child and thus to the reality of all death is not to be viewed as stoic resignation. . . .
>
> David had discerned, for whatever reasons, that the issues of his life are not to be found in cringing fear before the powers of death, but in his ability to embrace and abandon, to love and to leave; to take life as it comes, not with indifference but with freedom, not with callousness but with buoyancy.[12]

David's response to the child's death, not his illness, is to immediately sleep with Bathsheba who conceives Solomon. This is the freedom of the trusted creature.

The third incident concerns David and the water from the well at Bethlehem. The Philistines have occupied Bethlehem and David is encamped outside. In a moment of desire David sighs "Oh, if someone would fetch me a drink of water from the well that stands by the gate at Bethlehem." Three of his men hearing this request force their way through the Philistine camp and return with the water. When they give the water to David, he will not drink it. Instead he pours it on the ground as a libation. "Yahweh keep me from drinking this! This is the blood of men who went at the risk of their lives." David does not place himself above his men. He does not allow his kingship to separate him from the solidarity he has with all men. Water captured at the possible cost of life is for all to drink. The trusted creature is free to act beyond authority and rank.

It is the freedom of this man David to shape his own future and act in new and different ways that inspired the Yahwist to write the story of Adam. The inner energy of David's freedom was his belief that God believed in him. The world of David is not secular. He knows a transcendent God but far from oppressing him and keeping him in his place this God encourages him to find a place of his own. David celebrates life, takes responsibility, and risks decisions. He is what the human person looks like who lives through the breath God breathes into our nostrils.

The story now moves from the creation of the trusted creature to Incarnation of the Son. Although the incarnation stresses the presence of God in Jesus, it has always been held by the Church that the Son of God is truly man. The long geneology which begins the Gospel of Matthew attests to this humanity. One of the names on that list and consequently one of the titles of Jesus, one that is often overlooked, is Son of David. The trust and freedom which marked certain episodes in the life of David also permeates the story of Jesus. In parallel situations of holiness, death, and friendship Jesus acts with the freedom of the one trusted by God.

Jesus and his disciples are walking through the fields, picking corn on the Sabbath. The Pharisees complain that this activity is forbidden. Jesus recalls the David story and finishes with

"The Sabbath was made for man, not man for the Sabbath." What Jesus is rejecting, to return to our earlier discussion, is an exclusive Deuteronomic interpretation of the Sabbath. The Sabbath is a day of enforced rest because in the slavery of Egypt there was enforced work. Therefore the very fact of inactivity honors Yahweh's saving deed. What Jesus is affirming is the creation interpretation of Sabbath. The Sabbath is the sanctifying presence of God to all life. There is not one day which must be kept holy while all the others are "free" to be profane. God is not the jealous guardian of inactivity on one day but the gracious presence which urges men to be resourceful on all days. This incident is more than the breaking of custom. It proclaims a new understanding of the God-person relationship. God is not a law to be obeyed but a presence to be seized and acted on: humankind is not an obedient servant but free and resourceful people who get hungry even on the Sabbath.

The story of Jesus also shows a freedom with regard to death. However, unlike the David tale, Jesus' freedom is not in relation to the death of another (even a loved one) or death in the abstract but to his own impending death. Although the New Testament speaks of Jesus offering himself up, this does not mean that he courted death—a man with suicidal tendencies. Jesus' preaching, challenging so many of the assumptions of the power elite, marked him for a violent end. Jesus knew this but chose death rather than abandon his commitment to the Kingdom. This decision, described as the agony in the garden, has none of the ease of David's freedom. Jesus loved life. He was a man of table fellowship and banquet stories. Yet the insight seems to be that life can only be enjoyed when it is not clung to. Only with an allegiance to more than life is a person free within life. As the trusted one the power of death does not crush Jesus and force him to pass the cup. Freedom does not mean the denial of death but the refusal to allow it to determine life. What determines life is the trust that has been given.

Out of David's belief that Yahweh was committed to him he was able to relate in new ways to the situations that confronted him. Kingship did not lead to isolation and privilege. The water spilled on the ground is his solidarity with his men. The Johannine Jesus' consciousness of entrustment also leads to a new freedom.

> Jesus knew that the Father had *entrusted* everything into his hands, and that he had come from God and was returning to God, and he got up from the table, removed his outer garment and, taking a towel, wrapped it round his waist; he then poured water into a basin and began to wash the disciples' feet and to wipe them with the towel he was wearing.
> John 13:3-5

David will be equal with his men. The Son of God will serve his friends. Jesus' rootedness in God makes him capable of radical freedom. He can care beyond ego and rank. He can reverse the master-servant relationship and not feel his authority threatened. Further in the story, Peter refuses to have Jesus wash him. Jesus responds, "If I do not wash you, you can have nothing in common with me." What we want in common with Jesus is his relationship to God, for as John Fowler has remarked, "God is the freedom which makes all other freedoms possible."

In this unfolding of the story of Creation and Incarnation the Spirit of the Lord is the Spirit of freedom. "The Lord is the Spirit, and where the Spirit of the Lord is, there is freedom." What we are freed *from* is bondage to the law and the flesh and what we are freed for is a way of creatively belonging to each other. The law is a shorthand way of talking about a certain attitude toward the law. The law in itself is not enslaving but the way we relate to it often is. We use the law to prove ourselves, to justify our lives. In this situation we vacillate between arrogance when we are keeping the law and despair when its demands are beyond us. But the worst effect of this attitude is that our energy and effort are totally centered on ourselves. This is the link between bondage to the law and bondage to the flesh. The works of the flesh, as Paul lists them, may be immorality, impurity, licentiousness, idolatry, jealousy, anger, sorcery, enmity, strife, selfishness, dissension, envy, drunkenness, carousing (and the infamous ending) and the like but the organizing center of these activities is egoism. The law and the flesh are symbols of a self-preoccupation, an "incurvedness" as Martin Luther would have it, an arthritis of the soul, gnarled and bent, unable to stretch or touch—in a word, sin.

The Spirit which Jesus unleashes is the same sustaining breath which races through the nostrils of Adam. The Spirit brings freedom from self-preoccupation by establishing humankind as the trusted creature. The need to validate ourselves in an ultimate way and the fear we will not disappears before the Spirit-created consciousness that our self-worth is a gift of God. The unlimited anxiety we have about ourselves which is expressed in endless devotion to the ways of the flesh is relieved in the lived understanding that our security comes from beyond ourselves.

But the Spirit not only frees she also leads. Paul has other lists. One concerns the variety of the gifts of the Spirit: ". . . to one is given the utterance of wisdom . . . to another the utterance of knowledge . . . to another faith . . . to another healing . . . etc." (I Cor. 12:8-11). Another list itemizes the fruits of the Spirit: ". . . love, joy, peace, patience, kindness, goodness, trustfulness, gentleness, and self control" (Ga. 5:22). The gifts are not individual blessings but meant to build up the community. The fruits are not the property of individuals but the qualities that characterize the common life of the Church. If the Spirit was about individual improvement, egoism would still reign. The freedom which the Spirit brings is the freedom to pour water on the ground and wash the feet of your friends. It is the freedom to bind ourselves to each other in faith, hope, and love and so become the community who, when asked its identity, tells the story of Creation, Incarnation, and Spirit.

The story that Gn. 2 encourages complements the story line developed out of Gn. 1. The sanctifying presence of God to all created reality becomes the empowerment of the human person. The world of created dignity unfolds into the world of the trusted creature. The world of friendship and celebration unfolds into the world of sexuality and communion. The world of reverence and beauty unfolds into the world of freedom and solidarity. If people are the stories they tell, the people who tell the story of Creation, Incarnation, and Spirit are, most surely, a people of God.

Of course this is not enough. The appropriate setting for the tale so far is paradise and we live east of Eden. The story must include the episodes about the couple who clothe themselves because they are suspicious, about brothers who quarrel, betray, and kill, about the search through a whole city for one just man, and ultimately about a strange man on a cross and a people who resist any attempt to take him down. A story within a story must be told. The story of Creation, Incarnation, and Spirit is a skeleton: its heart is Fall, Crucifixion, and Church. This story within a story does not bring contradiction but explosion.

The larger story is shattered and then painfully pieced together. A radically new tale emerges, filled with terror and wonder. Yet the final feeling is that in some mysterious way it is the same story only more so. It creates the same world only now it is truly ours.

Fall, Crucifixion, and Church

We live, as the first chapter elaborated, in the environments of self, others, society, and universe and are related to a dimension of Mystery which permeates all these environments. Yet we experience all these relationships as estranged. The Mystery either recedes from our consciousness or, when it is strongly present, it appears indifferent to us. The universe in its immensity and unmanageability is threatening to us. In those areas which humankind has subdued, the universe threatens to exhaust itself and so leave us unsupported. The overarching institutions of society are not responsive to our needs. They have become dragons devouring individuals without conscience or care. At one time or another everyone has nodded to Sartre's insight that other people are hell. With their presence they bring guilt, anger, and suffocating obligation. And finally within myself I find alienation. Gide's remark, "I should like to ring true" and Chesterton's "Whoever I am, I am not myself," says it for us all.

Every view of man concedes that something is wrong.[13] And the wrong is not at the margins but at the core. Universe, society, and other people may be oppressors but the real predicament is deeper. It is reflected in the confession sequence from Leonard Bernstein's *Mass*.

> What I say I don't feel
> What I feel I don't show
> What I show isn't real
> What is real, Lord—I don't know,
> No, no, no—I don't know.
>
> I don't know why every time
> I find a new love I wind up destroying it.
> I don't know why I'm
> So freaky-minded, I keep on kind of enjoying it—
> Why I drift off to sleep
> With pledges of deep resolve again,
> Then along comes the day
> And suddenly they dissolve again—
> I don't know . . .
>
> What I need I don't have
> What I have I don't own
> What I own I don't want
> What I want, Lord, I don't know.

The predicament concerns the fundamental positioning of the self within the Mystery. This basic stance then expresses itself in the interpersonal, socio-political, and ecological relationships.

The Fall is the story that Christians tell to symbolize this in-depth experience of alienation. Although in Scripture Gn. 3-11 is a unit and so the Fall includes the stories of Cain and Abel, the Flood, and the Tower of Babel, it is the Adam and

Eve story which is the focal center. One major emphasis of the Adam and Eve story is that estrangement is the result of human freedom. The distortion which we experience is not a necessity but a perversion. There is nothing in the created order which encourages evil. The traditional interpretation of the snake as Satan obscures this point. The snake is not a subordinate principle of evil which tempts men but one of God's good creatures.[14] His presence deepens one mystery of evil rather than explains it. The mystery of evil demands the stark statement that estrangement comes about through the use of human freedom. Piet Hanema, a character in John Updike's novel, *Couples*, understands this.

> Things grow as well as rot. Life isn't downhill; it has ups and downs. Maybe the last second is up. Imagine being inside the womb—you couldn't imagine this world. Isn't anything's existing wonderfully strange? What impresses me isn't so much human self-deception as human ingenuity in creating unhappiness. We believe in it. Unhappiness is us. From Eden on, we've voted for it. We manufacture misery, and feed ourselves on poison. That doesn't mean the world isn't wonderful.[15]

Alienation is the result of how we relate ourselves to the creation we are and the creation we share.

To stop with the decisive role of human freedom in creating our experiences of estrangement is to tell only half a story. Freedom is not the cause of our distortedness but only the ability to distort. The fact that we are free to choose how we will relate to the existence we find ourselves within is the condition for estranged experiences but not the reason. The question of why we use freedom the way we do is the heart of the Fall. The most common interpretation is that disobedience caused the fall. God has given a command: Adam and Eve transgressed it. The source of all estrangement is disobedience. A second interpretation focuses not on the fact of a commandment but on its content. Adam and Eve were not to eat of the "tree of the knowledge of good and evil." "Good and evil" should not be considered in an exclusively moral sense but as "all things." Humankind is guilty of overreaching their limits, of trying to be divine and in the process becoming less than human. Pride is the source of our estranged experiences.

An interpretation which deepens disobedience and pride focuses on the attitude of trust. We attempt to move outside the Mystery when we cease to trust the Mystery we are within. The core of the temptation is the panicked feeling that creation is not good. Energy is not spent on creatively relating to the givens of life but on controlling them. We seek to be god because we have lost confidence in being a creature. And, of course, the depth of the perversion is that the god we seek to be is nothing like the real God. The heart of the matter is that the trusted creature does not trust.

The dynamics of estrangement spring from this fundamental fear-ridden, non-trusting stance. The general categories of Tillich are a helpful guide to this movement of alienation. The first moment consists in a turning away from God. We shrink from the givens and limits of life and from the impositions of the Mystery. We do not relate ourselves to God, earth, people, and society. In resisting an outward orientation we inevitably turn inward. We become our own center. Our created drive toward transcendence is twisted toward ourselves. Totally preoccupied with ourselves we try to draw all things into our world. We attempt to secure ourselves by ultimately investing in nation, race, wealth, etc. Yet all these things fail to fill the emptiness created by our initial rejection of Creation itself. Worse yet they paralyze us. Unable to secure our existence and unable to turn us toward God, they become gods.

> . . . idols are silver and gold,
> made by the hands of men.
> They have mouths that cannot speak
>   and eyes that cannot see;
> they have ears that cannot hear,
>   nostrils, and cannot smell;
> with their hands they cannot feel,
>   with their feet they cannot walk,
>   and no sound comes from their throats.
> Their makers grow to be like them,
> and so do all who trust in them.
>   Ps. 115:5-8
>   (New English Bible)

Not to trust in the Mystery does not mean that we have no God but that we have false gods. As Richard Niebuhr has suggested when the true

God is rejected the half-gods appear, and "when the half-gods go, the minimal gods arrive."[16]

This interpretation of the Fall focuses on the non-trusting way we relate to the givens of human existence. Yet there seems to be no evidence to encourage a trusting style. The particularity of birth, the aging process, the inevitability of suffering, the fact of death—none of these seem to manifest a graciousness which would elicit trust. In fact they seem to proclaim that reality, if not hostile, is indifferent and we should act accordingly. As the first chapter elaborated, our relationship to Mystery is ambiguous. At one moment it is funding our powers and at the next draining them. This commonplace experience suggests that life is out of control. Our only hope is not to trust the process but to fend it off.

The Wisdom tradition of Israel faced this problem. They tried to relate trust in Yahweh and his created order with the capriciousness of life in general and the fact of suffering in particular. This tradition believed that Yahweh ruled human life through an immanent order. The concept of Yahweh's interventionist activity, while always acknowledged, was not emphasized. The most recognized form of his presence was a pervasive wisdom which ensured the stability of the created order. This wisdom could be perceived and enunciated if one listened carefully enough, accumulated the evidence, and consulted the tradition. Therefore what connected the trustworthiness of Yahweh and his creation

with the untrustworthy tumult of experience was
insight. "For Israel, there was no insight which
did not imply trust, faith, but there was also no
faith which did not rest on insights."[17]

In general, two major responses to the mystery
of suffering developed in the Wisdom tradition.
The first was based on a firm belief in a cause
and effect structure, an act-consequence pattern. If suffering visited you, you had brought it
on your own head. A present punishment was a
sure sign of a past sin. This piece of wisdom is
deeply rooted in Jewish consciousness. The
friends of Job prosecute him to find the past
wrongdoing that has brought him to so pitiable a
state. When Joshua is defeated at Ai, he immediately suspects it is the result of sin and discovers
the thievery of Achan. The sailors who give
passage to Jonah know the storm is not arbitrary
and see its cause in the face of Jonah. By itself
this act-consequence portrayal of reality could
not handle the unevenness of experience. Evil
prospered and those who feared the Lord floun-
dered. To account for this the act-consequence
pattern developed a hope dimension. One could
never judge until the end was seen. The present
moment was never an accurate gauge of Yahweh's
justice.

> Do not grow heated at the wicked,
>   do not fly into a rage at the ungodly
> for the wicked man has no future,
>   the light of the ungodly goes out.
>   Prov. 24:19

If one were perceptive enough, the way in which the created order reenforced good and discouraged evil could be discovered.

A second response to the experience of seemingly gratuitous suffering was the idea of training. God sends sufferings, not because of previous sins, but because they are purgative and pedagogical.

> Yahweh's discipline, my son, do not refuse it . . .
> For who Yahweh loves, he rebukes,
>   and he allows the son whom he loves to suffer.
>   Prov. 3:11

> Gold is tested in fire,
>   but the man who pleases God in the furnace
>   of suffering.
>   Sir. 2:5

The persuasiveness of both these answers in their own day is debatable. The Book of Job (to a certain extent) and Ecclesiates (to a complete extent) abandon the attempt to insightfully square suffering with trust in God. The questions of Job are caught up in the majesty of God's creation but they are not answered. For Koheleth there is certainly a time for every purpose under heaven and a governing order. The problem is man does not know his time and he cannot discern the order.

Although today most people would quickly and often vehemently dismiss the act-consequence and training responses, there is a limited validity to each. These responses were never meant to be a total scheme of things, accounting for every experience of suffering. As partial insights they have a place. The notion of a pre-determined order external to human interaction and sustained by God which, when violated, returns the compliment does not reflect contemporary sensibilities. Acts have consequences but the connection is an inner logic not an inflexible order presided over by a moral God. A sinful act unfolds, spreads itself, is contagious. It creates destructive situations which, in turn, take on a life of their own and are quite oblivious of whom they engulf. We may balk at the idea of act-consequence but we relish the thought of poetic justice.

The notion of suffering sent by God to train (not to test) suggests a slightly sadistic God. Yet suffering, no matter what its origin, is a crucible. Many have held that it is the only path to compassion and love. Recognizing the inadequacy of all responses in this area, both of these fail to move us toward trust. One reason is that they were formulated within a theological framework too rigid to reflect the chaotic flow of historical living. Yet in one way their success or lack of it is not the point. The underlying faith intention is what must be credited. The wise men devoted their minds and energies to the everlasting task of not allowing the experiences of suffering to eclipse trust in the good creation of Yahweh.

The Cross of Christ can be interpreted as a

response to the question: How do we trust in a world distorted by our own betrayals and filled with deliberate sin and arbitrary suffering? The Cross is a symbol of deliberate sin and arbitrary suffering and on it is not just another hapless victim but the Son of God. The centurion in Mark's Gospel pronounces the deepest meaning of the cross, "Surely this was the Son of God." The Cross revolutionizes our understanding of God and presents to us new possibilities for life. God is not a heavenly King and the question is not how does he reward good and punish evil. God is a passionate presence to all human life, never deserting it. The Cross is the symbol of the fellow suffering of God. Elie Wiesel's story in *Night* is about this God.

> The SS hung two Jewish men and a boy before the assembled inhabitants of the camp. The men died quickly but the death struggle of the boy lasted half an hour. 'Where is God? Where is he?' a man behind me asked. As the boy, after a long time was still in agony on the rope, I heard the man cry again, 'Where is God now?' And I heard a voice within me answer, 'Here he is—he is hanging here on this gallows. . . .'[18]

The love of God demands he be wherever his creation is.

The Cross of Christ is the penetration of God into that unholy area where we would least expect him and, if the truth be known, where we least want him. God has entered into the loneliness of our suffering and the self-hatred of our sin.

And he has not come as judgment but as acceptance. The Cross is the communication of God's
care but it is not a message from the outside. God
loves us by receiving our lives into himself as we
experience them—torn and broken. The Cross is
God loving us from the inside. God has accepted
those aspects of our lives we ourselves have dis-
owned and denied. We fight the awareness of our
guilt, proving ourselves innocent at all costs. We
fear suffering and death so fiercely that it
dominates our imaginations and dictates to us the
shape of our days. If Creation is God's presence
to our beauty, the Cross is God's presence to our
pain and twistedness.

This accepting presence of God goes beyond
our carefully selective self-images. Implicitly or
explicitly we set up criteria of justification, qualities and attitudes through which we count ourselves worthwhile and without which we lose
value. These conditions of worth often work in a
defensive way. They screen out all experiences
and feelings that do not reenforce them. They
censor our relationships and lead us ever deeper
into self-deceit.

> In general, the person in self-deception is a person of
> whom it is a patent characteristic that even when
> normally appropriate he *persistently* avoids spelling-
> out some feature of his engagement in the world. . . .
> This inability to spell-out is not a lack of skill or
> strength; it the adherence to a policy (tacitly)
> adopted.[19]

If Augustine's insight that all sin is basically a lie is correct, every form of redemption must be an act of truth.

The Cross uncovers the deepest truth about the relationship of God and humankind. God is redemptively present to every moment of human life and therefore even in our sin and suffering we are not abandoned. God is intimately present to us and knows all we are. And knowing all we are he accepts us. This story of God disarms us. We were ready with conditions, conditions built on dishonesty, cover stories that hid our fear and malice and betrayals. But our doctored accounts are not needed before the crucified God. The viciousness with which we protect ourselves turns to calm before the graciousness of God. God's acceptance of even the worst in us has freed us from fear and without fear we do not need to lie. We can trust the long journey into ourselves and the Mystery of which we are a part.

This total acceptance by God and our response of trust does not encourage complacency but is the indispensable base of action. Without this grounding our energies are spent on stratagems of justification and protection. When the acceptance symbolized in the Cross suffuses our lives, we are freed to be for the other, to love in the same way we have been loved. This is the paradoxical message of Christianity. It is reflected not only in the Cross but in Jesus' Abba symbolism.

Its particularly paradoxical character consisted in this
that, whereas on one side of its expression it seemed
to favour quietism, on another side it demanded the
most active commitment. On one hand, people were
invited to cast their cares on a God whose minute
providence looked after the sparrows and the lilies,
even the hairs of their head, on the other hand they
were warned to count the cost before following in the
footsteps of this man of faith as carefully as if the
whole enterprise would depend on their efforts alone.
. . . Now we may notice that, out of this intense
acknowledgment of the Father-God, Jesus was capable
of declaring in word and deed (table fellowship with
outcasts and sinners, for instance), that God's forgive-
ness was freely available to all sinners. And the
paradox appears again. Whereas such a pronouncement might be expected to be followed by laxity of the
most enervating kind, Jesus clearly saw it not only to
be compatible with, but to be positively part of a
determination to change one's heart and to sin no
more.[20]

In the deep peace that acceptance brings, there
lives an imperative to change, a mission to share
what has been experienced.

In this story the Fall is not taken as a historical
event which changed the ontological structure of
reality. Correspondingly the Cross is not considered as a counter historical moment reestablish-
ing the ontological structure of the God-creation
relationship. The Fall is a symbolic rendering of
the estrangement we experience within created
existence. The Cross is a revelatory symbol of the
God-Creation relationship which reconstructs
consciousness and suggests a new way of re-

lating. As always, the human person who stands before the Cross is free. New consciousness, in itself, does not mean new life. Decision is the distinctive human trait.

To understand the Fall and the Cross symbolically and not as historical events is not an a-historical interpretation.[21] The Fall is about what we do with our historicity, with the freedom to determine our style of interaction with our environments. Also a symbolic understanding of Fall recognizes a "build-up" of non-trusting lives and so a real historical power which tries to force freedom in a single direction. The danger of this accumulated force of sinful precedents is that it obscures where the real decision lies. It presents "the fallen style" as a given, something which must be conformed to. The Cross reveals the possibility of living history in another way. In this story the Fall and Cross are about the ways of humankind in history but they are not investigated as specific historical events.

The Cross of Christ buys us back, not from the devil, but from the fear of created existence that told us not to trust and taught us how to lie. Through the Cross we do not trust because all danger has been removed. It has not been removed and never will be. Nor do we trust because in the last analysis God is in charge and everything will turn out right. Trust is neither safety in an unsafe world nor blindly held assurance in an ambiguous life. We trust created existence because there is no moment of it that is

not touched by the presence of God. Trust is a
personal relationship and the Cross reveals that
the person whom God wants to be related to
includes our weakness, the fact that we are
caught in sin and overwhelmed by suffering. Our
relationship to Mystery is reconfigured by the
symbol of the Cross and from it flows a new life,
not struggling to prove anything but to reflect its
reestablished vocation as the trusted creature.

The trust which the symbol of the Cross encourages is neither reliance nor safety nor pre-
sumption. It has absolutely no overtones of
passivity. The opposite of trust is not distrust but
fear. An old theological debate asks the question:
if Adam did not sin, would we have to die? One
answer to this question is a definite yes. Death is
the natural rhythm of created reality. What
would be missing if Adam had not sinned is the
overwhelming anxiety we bring to death. To trust
in created goodness is to move beyond debilitat-
ing anxiety. Trust does not shrink from the unavoidable demands of the Mystery, from relationship, sexuality, friendship, and social responsibility. On the other hand, fear is suspicious of
the very contours of life. To fear is to experience
the last covenant curse and think both waking
and dreaming are tricks. For the person who
lives within the Cross of Christ, trust is the God-
side of human courage.

Precise scriptural exegesis might place the
origin of the Church in the Easter experience or,

if they are to be distinguished, the Pentecost experience. But devotion suggests that the Church was born in the blood and water that flowed from the lanced side of the crucified Christ. Undoubtedly, Cross, Easter, and Pentecost represent a continuum of events which jointly could be called the birthday of the Church. Yet it is the cross which quickly becomes the center of Church life and piety. In fact, the earliest Gospel (Mark) has been characterized as a passion narrative with an extended introduction. The emphasis on the cross cannot be reduced to the fact that the early Christians were persecuted and that the suffering Christ both explained and supported their trials. The cross was more a theological embarrassment than a consolation. Why the Messiah had to die was a question the early Church continuously puzzled over. And death on a cross heightened the puzzle into a scandal. Yet it is this instrument of death that becomes the sign of his followers.

To explore the centrality of the cross for Church life it is not necessary to construct cosmic theories of atonement. Nor is it necessary to marshall scriptural texts to show why it had to be. It is enough to say that the cross so mysteriously touches who we are in relation to All There Is that it continues to evoke life and commitment. The cross can be considered as the supreme expression of human sinfulness. The drive is not only to kill the good but to kill the good God. It can also be seen as the summation of Jesus' life, bringing the questions of the Kingdom to their sharpest focus. But within the framework of our purposes the cross is a story of God. It stands at the center of the Christian community not only as a reminder of human sinfulness and the dedication of Jesus but as the revelation of the God who is intrinsic to the identity and life of the Church.

The cross is the grounding of the Christian community, its symbol of realism, and its ongoing principle of critique. It is often noted that ecclesiology has its roots in Christology but it is often overlooked that Christology brings us back to theology. The foundation of the Church is the experience of God symbolized in the crucified Christ. The cross reveals God's self-giving love which frees us from our self-serving apathy. Out of God's total acceptance comes the freedom and power to form community, to belong to each other in a life-giving way. God has taken into himself all that is worst about us and turned it toward good. The law of the cross is not that evil has been eliminated but that it has been transformed into possibility. The power of sin and suffering which generated the anti-community styles of domination, manipulation, and deceit has been broken. If we dwell within the cross of Christ, the compulsion to protect ourselves at all cost yields to the possibilities of dialogue, respect, and integrity. The funding experience which makes

Christian community possible is the God on the cross.

The cross also symbolizes the realism which must characterize Christian life. If God's freeing presence to us involved entering into our sin and suffering, our freeing presence to each other will involve no less. To pursue a life of trust, friendship, and justice is to follow the discipleship of the cross. In the concrete world in which we live, the trusted creature is often the suffering creature; the one who is responsible is the one who risks his life. The Christian eucharist reflects this understanding. The bread and wine are symbols of all God's gifts. The meal is the expression of sacred friendship and community. Yet the bread is a body broken, the wine a blood outpoured, and the meal a sacrifice. The way of community entails suffering love, love willing to give itself. Dostoevsky's remark that love in reality is a "harsh and dreadful thing" might be too strong. But love does demand sacrifice. The Christian community which is sustained by the God on the cross is not tempted to love in dreams.

God on the cross not only funds the Christian community and holds it to the concrete demands of love but also presents an everlasting, transcendent critique. The reality of God has always been considered the source of power. If true power hangs on a cross, it is in blatant opposition to all false power which puts people on crosses.

If the authority of God is self-giving love which makes possible community, it undercuts authority which works out of self-protecting fear. The God on the cross will not sanction our manipulating ways and dominating styles. The facile wisdom that power is for control and muscle makes community is folly before the cross. Vulnerability is what binds us together, not the vulnerability of the timid and the frightened but the vulnerability of those who care, the vulnerability of the God on the cross. Before the God on the cross our strivings for total control and absolute power are unmasked for what they are: fear of life. In the unmasking we belong to each other.

The story of Fall, Crucifixion, Church sets within the story of Creation, Incarnation, Spirit and reaffirms its basic thrust only now in the face of the mystery of sin and evil. The sanctifying presence of God to all human life does not withdraw when we spurn it. Just the opposite, it pursues us. The created dignity which is ours is appropriated in a new way. We are not paradisiacal innocents but broken people who have found the source of healing. Our basic relational stance within the Mystery we participate in is trust, but it is a trust shot through with fear. But the fear will not turn us to stone for in the middle of our fear is the crucified presence of God. We live in friendship mixed with betrayal, sexuality mixed with disrespect, community mixed with factionalism. But the God of the garden and the

cross is freeing us for new life within these relationships. To tell the story of Creation, Incarnation, Spirit and Fall, Crucifixion, Church is to live
in the world of trust and freedom.

The Johannine Jesus said, "Peace is my parting
gift to you, my own peace, such as the world
cannot give. Set your troubled hearts at rest, and
banish your fears." To tell the story of trust and
freedom is to live in that peace.

CHAPTER FIVE

A Story of Invitation and Decision

"Theology is very old ice cream, very tame sausage."[1]
Lawrence Durrell

"Poetry is quick as tigers, clever as cats, vivid as oranges."[2]
Delmore Schwartz

IN THE STORIES OF HOPE and justice and trust and freedom God was often portrayed as the lead actor. The Creator God kneaded the earth; the Warrior God smote the Egyptians; the Father God sent his Son. His acts gathered and scattered men and the stories unfolded in terms of his angers and delights. It seemed that Bultmann's definition of myth was perfect: "Myth gives worldly objectivity to that which is otherworldly."[3] When God is portrayed as a character, the story is concrete, vivid, and engaging. It is closer to truth than hyperbole to say that wherever the religious imagination is alive, God walks in the cool of the garden, consults with his prophets, and breaks the tombs of his friends.

Our interpretation did not read the stories as descriptive accounts of God activities. They were not meant to point to a separate entity called God and detail his movements. The figure of God revealed the transcendent meaning of our relationship to Mystery and so created a habitable world. Yet even with this caution there is a dys-

functional aspect to picturing God as a character.
Once the imagination pictures God as a supreme
being over-against us, our sensitivities are geared
for intervention. Unless God walks through the
door, he is not there. The universal presence of
God is overlooked while we scan the horizon for a
particular intervention. This is not a question of
either the existence of activity of God but a
recognition of the limits of religious imagination.

An alternate portrayal of God in the stories of
hope and justice and trust and freedom was not
as one of the cast but as a presence to all the
cast. God is the context, that reality before whom
life is lived, the ensurer of order and stability.
Brian Wicker notes this change of roles.

> . . . in the New Testament, God does not figure as a
> character in the stories. He is implicit, hidden,
> present in the wings but never on stage. He is not
> named. He is simply 'the Father' etc. He is present
> only as related to human characters, not as a char-
> acter in his own right. He intervenes only indirectly,
> through Jesus or through those ordinary men to whom
> he entrusts special powers, as recorded in the Acts of
> the Apostles. His spirit is at work, but he is not
> present in person. He is available only indirectly in
> Jesus the man whose personality reveals, in a glass
> darkly, something of his 'character'.[4]

Not only in the New Testament but also in the
David stories God's role is simply to be there. He
is the guarantor of the processes of life which
have their own rhythms and laws. He does not

interrupt them. "He is much more the *creator of a context* for human freedom and responsibility than a *disrupter of events.*"[5]

But presence, even a presence that insures an orderly outcome to a disorderly history, tends to become aloof. A presence that oversees is not far from a cold stare. If intervention tends to be the way the character God contacts men, logic would seem to be the way men would contact the non-acting presence of God. God as a pervasive presence leaves the human person free to enact her own future but the haunting question is: does it leave her completely alone? The suspicion is that a God whose very life is not bound with ours might not care.

The story of invitation and decision is the cumulative tale that the parables and some of the sayings of Jesus unfold. In the parables God is not imagined as the lead character or as a background presence. God is the plot. God is what happens to the people in the story or to the people hearing the story. As plot the God of the parables is himself invisible. He is the summer God. "Take the fig tree as a parable: as soon as its twigs grow supple and its leaves come out, you know that summer is near" (Mk. 13:28). No one has seen summer yet its presence is proclaimed by the budding tree. No one has seen God yet his presence is proclaimed by the transformed person. A poem in Kazantzakis' *Report to Greco* trades on Jesus' parable.

I said to the almond tree,
'Sister, speak to me of God.'
And the almond tree blossomed.[6]

In any story, character and plot cannot be arbitrarily separated. We are interested in people because of what they are undergoing and what people are undergoing changes their character. In the parables people are undergoing God. The concern of the story of invitation and decision is neither people nor God but the *movement* of God in people and *movement* of people in God. The juxtaposition of the two introductory quotes attempts to highlight this. Too often theology isolates God and becomes old and tame talk about a distant being. But poetry, the poetry of the sayings and parables of Jesus, is not about something over there but is the experience of the quickening touch of what is present. The dynamic interpenetration of God and person is crucial.

Without the emphasis on movement and interchange the components of the story separate and harden. The people component becomes prey to either sentimentality or disdain. Flannery O'Connor once remarked that sentimentality is giving more tenderness to things than God does. People are coddled; tears do not lead to resolve. Disdain is the opposite extreme. It is the cynical remove of the heart from the struggling process of being human. It is a haughty spirit which has no tears to give. On the other hand, the divine component is often corrupted into magic or gnosis. The effort is to control God for our own purposes or to rarify and restrict him to "those who know." Martin Buber cites these two dangers.

> The two spiritual powers of gnosis and magic, masquerading under the cloak of religion, threaten more than any other powers the insight into the religious reality, into man's dialogical situation. They do not attack religion from the outside; they penetrate into religion, and once inside it, pretend to be its essence. [7]

When God is portrayed as the plot of the story, the interactional flow of the divine and human components is stylistically established.

Although the parables concern the movement of God, they focus on the catalytic elements in the process rather than the larger context. The larger context is the central motif of Jesus' preaching, the Kingdom of God. If the Kingdom of God is not a living symbol in the imaginative life of the people, the parables do not have a receptive atmosphere. They are disengaged from their life-giving ecology and become isolated exercises in storytelling. Both Norman Perrin and Amos Wilder stress this point.

> Now if the parable is to function effectively as a parable *of the Kingdom of God*, then clearly it can so function only if the myth of God active as king is also functioning. Jesus addressed his parables to people who fully accepted the myth and so his parables were effective forms of proclamation of the Kingdom, or of instruction with regard to response to the proclamation. [8]

His parables alone, even with the life of action which
framed them, would have been ambiguous without the
prior mythical horizon of the kingdom of God as he
announced it, so also evoking the basic orientation of
the people.[9]

The Kingdom of God establishes the "answering
imagination."[10] to the parables. Without it the
stories become examples and allegories but not
invitations into the life of God.

The Kingdom of God, as the quote from Norman
Perrin suggests, is a symbol evoking a myth. The
phrase is a shorthand way of bringing to consciousness a larger vision of reality. It functions
in this way only for the community who truly
owns the symbol. Kingdom of God is not an
archytypal symbol with universal resonance but
is limited to a definite cultural group. It belongs
to Hebrew and Christian history and its ability to
immediately and powerfully communicate a vision
of reality is restricted to the peoples of those
communities. In Christian history, Kingdom of
God has evoked many different visions. At one
time it brought to mind the hope for life after
death; at another time it reflected the hierarchial
Church and its sacramental system. For Jesus it
evoked the vision that God was active as King on
behalf of his people.

> . . . the primary and essential reference is to the
> sovereignty of God conceived of in the most concrete
> possible manner, i.e. to his *activity* in ruling. . . . The
> Kingdom of God is the power of God expressed in
> deeds; it is that which God does wherein it becomes
> evident that he is king. It is not a place or community

> ruled by God; it is not even the abstract idea of reign
> or kingship of God. . . . The kingdom of God is, of
> course, for the Jew an everlasting Kingdom: God
> always was, is, and always will be king, and the
> activity wherein he manifests himself as such is ever-
> lastingly to be experienced and expected.[11]

A vision of God active in human life is the home of the parables.

If we are to tell the parables so that they are stories of God, we must have some understanding of divine activity in human life. The fact that the symbol "God acts" befuddles many people is not due to the lack of models.[12] The ancient monarchial model envisions God as absolute ruler of his creation. He totally controls all events and destinies. The problems of theodicy, why does the good God allow evil, and the questions of predestination and freedom haunt this model. A second model sees God as the master clockmaker who wound the world into motion, supplied predictable laws, and retired. This deist understanding restricts God to originating activity. A third model applies the dynamics of interpersonal relationships to the relationship with God. God and the humn person are engaged in an I-Thou dialogue. God is the Thou that can never be an It (Buber) and so our relationship is always personal. A fourth model draws its analogy from human actions. A human action is more than a bodily movement. A bodily movement (raising my arm) can mean many things (stretching, waving hello, etc.). It becomes a human action when it is specified by intention. In a similar way, God's action is focused in terms of his intention. The movements of history and nature, therefore, can only be understood as divine activity when God's intention for them is revealed. Certain events, e.g. Jesus Christ, are especially expressive of God's intention and so provide clues to his universal activity.

The most promising model of God's activity is developed from process philosophy. God's relationship to the world is viewed as the preeminent member of a community to the entire community. Between God and the world there is mutuality and interdependency. God acts in the world only in cooperation with other entities. Neither God nor the world act independently. The unit of activity is God-World. God is the ground of both order and novelty. He not only structures the possible forms of relationships but presents novel possibilities to those relationships. God has an initial aim for every moment of experience. Human freedom responds to and actualizes that aim to the extent that it is willing and able. God then becomes the lure, the evocation toward the increase of value. God is not a monarch but a fellow sufferer, not a tyrant but a loving parent who encourages but never forces. The human person is the co-creator of every moment.

These models differ from one another and have both strengths and weaknesses. The monarchial model has a firm sense of transcendence but jeopardizes human freedom. The deistic model accounts for God's relationship to nature in a Newtonian way but neglects his relationship to people. The dialogic reverses the deistic, stressing the personal and slighting nature. The agent model offers an overall understanding but has trouble finding a significant place for the human contribution. The process model is the most comprehensive but it has been questioned whether the God of this model inspires worship and commitment.

Although the models are different in content and scope, they are formally the same. They are logical abstractions. They conceive of God and world as discrete entities and procede to speculate on how they could interrelate without compromising their distinctive features. What results is an intelligible construction without immediate existential import. Only with difficulty and heightened ambiguity can concrete historical events be cited as evidence of God's monarchial, deistic, dialogical, intentional, or processive activity.

After David Griffin elaborates a coherent account of revelation using the process model, he notes its limits: "The issue here is not, of course, whether these conditions could be verified, but only whether an intelligible conceptualization of an affirmation that might be believed is possible."[13] The models help untangle the mental processes but the naming of divine activity in a particular concrete event is still elusive.

The thought of James Mackay does not put forward another model of divine-human interaction but offers a fresh approach to the symbol "God act."[14] This approach is both sympathetic with the anthropology sketched in chapter one and provides a supportive context for telling parables. For Mackay the traditional contrasting of faith and reason is wrongheaded. In fact this "pitting against" has possibly done more harm to religious people than repressive ecclesiastical structures and obsolete liturgical practices. It implies that faith is not reasonable and that it is, in some way, outside the realm of the human spirit. Mackay argues that faith must be granted equal citizenship in the city of the human. Faith is one of the ways the human spirit relates to reality and reality to the human spirit. It stands side by side with science, art, and morality and cannot be reduced to any of them. Although these various approaches are interrelated, they are internally autonomous. Faith is a natural and ir-reducible human enterprise.

Faith is the acknowledgment of a Creative Will in and behind empirical reality. This acknowledgement is provoked by the inner dynamics of creaturely existence.

> I become aware that I and my world exist, miracu-lously exist. They do not found this existence them-selves, and they cannot guarantee it. I am unex-pectedly alive: always threatened with non-existence, yet positively, at first inexplicably existing. Within that awareness, whether it be an unreflective aware-ness of my own, or one very much explicated for me by the reflective analysis of a Tillich, lies for me the possibility, my possibility of acknowledging a creative will on which my life depends.[15]

Another approach is to realize that life, the very contingency we are, is an invitation which we may either accept or refuse. "In the last analysis the difference here is not between responding to an invitation or not, it is the difference between seeing existence, life as an invitation and seeing it as absurd, offensive to the human mind."[16] An existence which is given but not guaranteed is a sustained invitation.

Although the acknowledgment of a Creative Will reflects the Catholic sensibilities of a natural theology, it is not a proof of God. We cannot disengage ourselves from existence in order to approach it neutrally. In this dimension of human experiencing the "step back" track of the mind is misleading. The word is not *knowledge,* the result of objective data and impersonal evidence, but *acknowledge,* the result of address and response. Acknowledge moves beyond accurate information to entail the relational feelings of hope, love, and trust. In Mackay's thought this acknowledgment is prior to and the real grounding for any "proof of God."

> The proofs of God are, rather, reflective presentations of a spontaneous, prereflective insight or conviction of the human spirit that involved in this contingent existence—however the contingency is felt in the concrete; in change, birth and death, order and the break down of order—there is a Creative Will.[17]

Faith is the word for the human spirit's natural acknowledgment of God.

The person who relates to reality through faith encounters events and people which startle, deepen, and reconfigure his faith. When this

occurs, the religious person often uses revelational language to uncover its deepest meaning.
The person does not say, "I believe God is active
here." Instead he moves to the divine point of
view and says, "God is active here." Although
this move adds nothing new to the experience of
religious faith, it is both necessary and appropriate. Only revelational language expresses the
intensity of the faith conviction. It is a natural
transition within the language of faith.

> If I acknowledge God, the creative will both beyond
> and in the universe, both transcendent and immanent,
> that very acknowledgment naturally translates itself
> into affirmations that God is active in this historical
> world, particularly in its key events, more particularly
> still in those events which have significance for the
> future of religious belief, most particularly of all in the
> people at the centre of such events, the people whose
> events, in a very real sense they are. The moment the
> language of faith (that is, language which involves the
> characteristic words of that category of psychic
> behaviour, such as acknowledge, belief etc.), trans-
> lates, as it naturally does, into the languge of affirma-
> tion, one finds oneself speaking from God's point of
> view, and very shortly after that one is into the
> category of revelation.[18]

Also the foundational concern of the religious
person is to lead his life in the light of his faith
conviction. He wishes to understand God's intention so that he can commit himself to God's
future. Revelational language performs this expressive and concrete task. The stories of hope

and justice and trust and freedom were examples of this process. They revealed God's intention so the people who told them could relate to it.

James Mackey has instigated a Copernican revolution. He has reversed the revelation-faith procedure. God reveals himself, the traditional order asserts, and then we respond in faith. In this line-up, energy is focused on finding genuinely disclosive events and protecting them from the infringement of psychology, science, and history. Is God acting here or is it only man and how do we tell the difference? In Mackay's scheme faith is first-order language and revelational language, necessarily flowing from faith, is second-order language. Mackay asks for a reverent agnosticism.

> It is truly amazing that this kind of agnosticism is not found more generally acceptable, or more widely and consistently acknowledged. If one accepts the almost extreme agnosticism with regard to God's nature which Aquinas, for example, admits . . . why should one not accept at least an equal agnosticism with regard to God's actions? *Actio sequitur esse*, as the Scholastics used to say. More popularly put, the point would read: if the nature of a thing is known from its activity—and that is surely true in all cases—then it cannot be possible to claim to know more about the actions of something than one can know about its nature. Yet the very people who will admit that we know that God is but not what he is, immediately proceed to say with the utmost confidence that God acted with such intention at such a point in history or even in their own lives.[19]

To talk about divine activity is not to hunt for supernatural inputs or to detect that "something extra" in the situation. Language about God's activity discloses the significance of those encounters which have inspired us "to believe, or to believe once again, or to believe with a new intensity or a new direction in life."[20] It should be immediately suspected that any understanding which makes the last first and the first last would be sympathetic horizon for parabolical storytelling.

Mackay's thought gives coherent expression to how God functions as plot. Many of the parables are about intense human activity, crisis moments of panic and resolve. There is beauty in the parables but very little of the sublime. The cast of characters are the ordinary run of people: cheating accountants, longing fathers, grumbling workers, pleading widows, demanding friends, arrogant clerics, joyous farmers, wily servants, frantic housewives, beaten men, murdering tenants, and clever schemers. Yet both the people within the story and the people hearing the story do not remain on the level of the everyday. They are "thrown back" into their fundamental relationship to Mystery. If our relationship to Mystery often appears static, the parables reveal its dynamism. If our relationship to Mystery often seems dispensable or compartmentalized, the parables show how it sweeps us along and penetrates to our inner being. When

the parables function as catalysts for the basic
faith relationship to God, we naturally speak of
God's activity. The parables are stories about
people. But because of what is happening to the
people in the parables and to the people hearing
the parables they are also stories of God.

The Kingdom of God symbolizes divine activity
in human life which, in turn, directs attention to
those people and events which stimulate our
acknowledgment of a Creative Will. This stimula-
tion is not merely an intellectual "shaking up."
Our relationship to God is always a redemptive
process. When people and events trigger a transition from situations, attitudes, and behaviors
which can be characterized as diabolic (tearing
apart) to situations, attitudes, and behaviors
which can be characterized as symbolic (putting
together), we speak of God actively present in our
lives. In this movement the question of who is
guilty for the sinful situation is not pursued. All
that is recognized is the destructiveness of the
prevailing conditions and the chance to change
them. The parables are interested in possibility
not culpability. Our previous stories of God which
revealed his intentions provide the content of the
redemptive movement. When we are moving from
despair to hope, from exploitation to justice, from
fear to trust, from slavery to freedom, the leaven
God is present. "The Kingdom of God . . . is like
the yeast a woman took and mixed in with three
measures of flour till it was leavened all through"

(Luke 13:21). The leaven is hidden. Who sees it? Yet when the bread rises, we acknowledge that it is there.

The parables focus on the movement from sin to redemption. They are imaginative sketches which portray the catalytic elements of grace and decision. We move out of situations, attitudes, and behaviors that are destructive because something happens to us. We are gifted. Suddenly someone or something appears in our world and invites us out. The logic of our situation is broken. In farming a barren field a treasure is stumbled upon; a corner is turned and the perfect pearl is for sale: out of nowhere comes an invitation to the King's party. In parables, conjunctions are not the favorite part of speech. The parables are not smooth stories but the interruption of smooth stories by sudden possibility. But in the face of possibility, we must choose; in the face of invitation, we must decide. Our lives are not accurately described by the mechanical "already and not yet." The real poles are "is not and may not be." The full movement of God only occurs when freedom seizes it. Our relationship to Mystery is an ongoing redemptive process which lines up: sin—grace—decision—redemption.

Within this larger context the parables explore the invitation-decision dynamic. Some parables function as similes and others as metaphors. A simile is governed by the comparative "like;" a metaphor is characterized by the predicate "is."

The simile-parable illustrates the invitation-decision moment. It presents a pattern with the suggestion that it be used to investigate your own experiences. In the simile-parable a second movement is required. There must be an imaginative transference from story to life. In the metaphor-parable the story is life. The hearer is pulled into the tale and participates in its reality. Metaphor-parable is unfinished until the hearer has responded. There is no need to apply the story for the story is its own application. To listen to the story is to experience invitation and decision.

It seems there cannot be a hard and fast classification of the parables into simile and metaphor. Whether a parable is a simile or a metaphor cannot be settled in the abstract. The same parable may function as a metaphor for one person and a simile for another. Since the response of the hearer is integral to the parable, he will determine to a large extent how it functions. For the people of Jesus' time the parable of the sower might have pulled them into the story and, once inside, precipitated the experience of God's gift of life. The experience of hearing the parable *was* the experience of the Kingdom. For modern urban dwellers the same parable might function as a simile. Hearing the parable would not mean experiencing the Kingdom but learning how the Kingdom is experienced. The pattern is that the Kingdom comes as gift and surprise. Through the story then the hearer becomes sensi-

tized to the gift dimension of life itself and the
various particular gifts he has received. In a
simile experience the parable does not draw the
person in; the person draws the parable out.

Although the exact functioning of the parable
depends on its setting, some of the parables of
Jesus have enduring metaphoric power. The
stories of Jesus are concrete and situated,
detailing the everyday life of first century Palestine. Yet their particularity is not always an
isolating factor. Many parables are specific
appropriations of universal situations and so they
have intuitive resonance for other cultures and
other times. Few people stay outside the stories
of the Prodigal Son, the Vineyard Workers, and
the Good Samaritan. They might not enter the
stories in the same way as the Jews of Jesus' time
but they do enter the story. These stories reflect
the universal situations of family, work, and helplessness in such a way that the hearer becomes
participant within the story and is invited to
decide.

But whether the parables of Jesus function as
metaphor or simile, their common concern is the
actual life of the hearer. Their purpose is to
invite the hearer out of his present destructiveness and make possible new life. Whether this
existential reality occurs *within* the story or
occurs through the story as it focuses the
hearer's life is an interesting but secondary
consideration. The parables are both about

divine activity in human life (the Kingdom of God) and the actual experiencing of divine activity.

In order to understand the unique and powerful way the parables invite, the depth of the situation of sin must be explored. Every attitude and behavior is grounded in a vision of reality. We work out of preconceptions, unexamined biases which encourage certain attitudes and behaviors and forbid others. Although our specific projects often appear theory-free, they are really instances of an overall direction, a personal policy to which we implicity adhere. Put in another way, every person has a faith, a set of presuppositions which are tested out in everyday life. If this foundational structure is too constricted or self-centered, a crippling lifestyle develops. Attitudes and behaviors become destructive of both self and community. The depth of sin, therefore, is not in the destructive activity itself but in the consciousness which encourages and validates that activity.

Parables take aim at these presuppositions and dominant directions. Their goal is subversion. They are meant to penetrate to the core of what we unquestionably hold and question it. In the realm of parable nothing is safe. The God who happens in parables heals but does not facilely answer. The Tillichian correlation is strangely twisted back on itself. God is the answer to the question which is human existence. But a transcendent God is an answer in such a way that he continually keeps the question alive. The much vaunted image of the human being as a searcher is only a partial picture. We have many answers, prescribed solutions to the problems of life, proverbial remedies for any situation, but the God of the parables is the answer who questions all of them.

When the stories function parabolically, the result is imaginative shock. The story cracks open an enclosed world and issues a frightening invitation to "go beyond." Dominic Crossan has skillfully outlined the parabolic nature of the Old Testament story of Jonah.[21] The unquestioned assumption of the Jews of that time is that prophets hear the word of God and obey it and pagans do not. Yet the story is about a prophet who hears the word of God and disobeys it ("Jonah decided to run away from Yahweh.") and pagans who hear the word of God and obey it ("The news reached the King of Nineveh, who rose from his throne, took off his robe, put on sackcloth and sat down in ashes."). The story reverses expectations and shatters the simplistic and moralistic world of Jew-pagan prejudices. Out of the ruins comes an invitation to a new world.

A large part of the power of the parable is that you do not see it coming. Parable is blind side storytelling. It is Nathan telling David a story about a rich and unscrupulous man who took the last sheep of a poor shepherd. Nathan allows David to be outraged by the tale before he knifes

him with the conclusion that he is the man.
Robert Funk has a few theses:

1. Grace always wounds from behind, at the point
   where man thinks he is least vulnerable.
2. Grace is harder than man thinks: he moralizes
   judgment in order to take the edge off it.
3. Grace is more indulgent than man thinks: but it is
   never indulgent at the point where he thinks it
   ought to be indulgent.[22]

The parables are rooted in the Kingdom of God
and so respect the created dignity of each
person. But they do not respect us in the fanta-
sized and distorted ways we respect ourselves. In
that lies their power and their danger.

One of the most studied parables of recent
times is the Good Samaritan.[23] The story is told to
an audience for whom the Samaritan is an ir-
redeemable outcast. According to some Rabbis,
for a Jew to accept alms from a Samaritan
delayed the coming of the Kingdom. Although
there are varying interpretations of this parable,
they agree that the parable functions meta-
phorically and concerns the "clash of worlds."
In Crossan's interpretation the parable ends with
the question addressed to the hearer: "Which of
the three proved neighbor to the man who fell
among robbers?" The Jew is forced to put together two words which were previously un-
thinkable—Samaritan and neighbor.[24] Crossan
characterizes this as a reversal parable for
"when good (clerics) and bad (Samaritan) be-

come, respectively, bad and good, a world is being challenged and we are faced with polar reversal."[25] The automatic world of good and bad is challenged and in the challenge the Kingdom is experienced.

Robert Funk's interpretation also involves the hearer but not by urging him toward the shocking phrase, good Samaritan. For Funk the hearer identifies with the man in the ditch. "The future which the parable discloses is the future of every hearer who grasps and is grasped by his position in the ditch."[26] The victim is without name and face and so the hearer automatically supplies his own. The hearer as victim sees the world much differently than he ordinarily does. The respected priest and Levite pass him by and the hated Samaritan helps him beyond belief.

> He went up and bandaged his wounds, pouring oil and wine on them. He then lifted him on to his own mount, carried him to the inn and looked after him. Next day, he took out two denarii and handed them to the inn-keeper. 'Look after him,' he said, 'and on my way back I will make good any extra expense you have.'
>
> Luke 10:34-36

The hearer is left shocked and disoriented. Which world is the real one—the world of his everyday assumptions or the world he has discovered in his parabolic identity as victim?

Robert Tannehill suggests that the hearer will not identify with the man in the ditch but with his rescuer. In the structure of the parable the

hearer expects the third passer-by to help and he
is geared to relate to him. When it is the Samaritan who arrives, this anticipated identity takes
an unexpected turn.

> He [Samaritan] is clearly the hero, and yet the story
> makes it brutally hard for the audience to identify with
> him. He appears now not as the representative of their
> goodness but as representative of an alien goodness.
> He is an alien, for he steps across the boundaries
> which men put around their love. [27]

No matter what interpretation is preferred, the
historical thrust of the parable was to infiltrate
prejudices and subvert them.

Imaginative shock is not restricted to the parables. Many of the sayings of Jesus also use this
tactic.[28]

> If anyone hits you on the right cheek, offer him the
> other as well; if a man takes you to law and would
> have your tunic, let him have your cloak as well. And
> if anyone orders you to go one mile, go two miles with
> him. Give to anyone who asks, and if anyone wants to
> borrow, do not turn away.
>
> Matt. 5:39b-42

These extreme statements are not literal guides
for behavior. They are imaginative indictments of
our natural tendency to put ourselves first. These
statements do not fit into our world of excessive
self-concern. They force us to question what
seems so obvious and the questioning is the
beginning of an invitation.

> You know that among the pagans their so-called rulers
> lord it over them, and their great men make their
> authority felt. This is not to happen among you. No;
> anyone who wants to be first among you must be slave
> to all.
>
> Mark 10:42-44

This language also reverses worlds. We know
only too well about rulers but there is no place in
our world for rulers who are servants. Our basic
criteria of greatness will have to shift in order to
accommodate this language. Jesus' sayings over-
turn our normal ideas of power and prestige.

When the parables and sayings of Jesus function as imaginative shock, they result in the hearer's perceptual shift. What happens is that the
person sees herself and her situation in a new
way. This shift does not mean just one more
option. It creates a different reality with different
possibilities. The parables do not produce new
input or better ideas. They do not change the
content of thought but the framework with which
one thinks. This new framework is both continuous and discontinuous with the framework
which structured consciousness previous to hearing the parable. What is continuous is the foundational elements of the situation (Samaritan-
Jew). What is discontinuous is the configuration
of the relationship. If the parables and sayings of
Jesus are taken as a clue, perceptual shift is the
Christian process of growth.

Perceptual shift is not an isolated event of
consciousness transformation. It immediately
leans toward action. The first desire is to seize

and own the new world the parable has made possible. The urgency to act is the message of many of Jesus' parables. The unjust steward who, hearing he is going to be fired, doctors his master's accounts in order to secure another job is commended precisely because he acted. The point does not concern morality but apathy. Here is a man who finds himself in a crisis and, instead of wallowing in self-pity, acts resourcefully. The guests who do not respond to the King's banquet are quickly rejected and others are summoned. Immediate response is the mood of the Kingdom. Imaginative shock issues an invitation which leads to decision and action.

The action which the parables urge is openended. The parable attacks at the foundational level. They do not aim at particular activities but the visions of reality which undergird those activities. Therefore the need to decide and act is more a general command than a series of concrete proposals. The awareness is: if the new world is not concretely enacted, the old will reclaim consciousness. What is appropriate behavior after parable contact can be only generically spelled out. To use our previous stories as guides, parables which subvert our worlds of apathy, injustice, fear, and bondage would yield styles of hope, justice, trust, and freedom. Dominic Crossan succinctly distinguishes the call to action from its content. "Jesus' parables challenge one to life and action within the Kingdom but they leave that life and that action as absolute in its call as it is unspecified in

its detail."[29] Invitation means decision and action
but the shape of action will depend on our crea-
tivity and the demands of the situation.

When the parables of Jesus function as metaphor, they are powerful stories which touch and
realign our foundational loyalties and convictions. When they function as simile, they serve
the natural faith of the Christian in another way.
They are now illustrations of the redemptive
process. They detail what people look like in the
throes of conversation. Therefore a pattern can
be abstracted from the story and used as a
"watching brief"[30] both for human experience
and other stories. The pattern becomes a way to
get a fix on the redemptive activity of God in
human life and a way of discerning contemporary
stories of God. For many today, the parables
themselves are not the experience of the Kingdom
but the way we become sensitive to the contemporary presence of the Kingdom.

The parabolic pattern, the depth dynamics of
the process of grace and decision, can be drawn
from the parables of the treasure and the pearl.

> The Kingdom of heaven is like treasure hidden in a
> field which someone has found; he hides it again, goes
> off happy, sells everything he owns and buys the field.
> Again, the kingdom of heaven is like a merchant
> looking for fine pearls; when he finds one of great
> value, he goes and sells everything he owns and buys
> it.
>
> Matt. 13:44-46

Dominic Crossan sees in these parables the structure of the experience of the Kingdom.[31] A man suddenly *finds* a treasure. Something enters his life he had not planned, for he was not treasure hunting but farming. Overjoyed by the find, he willingly *sells* what he has. All that he owns does not compare with what he has found. He seizes this new-found gift and *buys* the field. The parable of the pearl reveals the same pattern of finding, selling, buying. This pattern provides a way to investigate personal experience and other stories.

When a Christian appropriates his life through the parables of Jesus, he is sensitive to what he is finding, selling, and buying. He recognizes the inescapable interrelatedness of existence and the ways in which people are present to each other. He knows gifts appear unbidden and unexpected and that some are bread and fish and some are stones and serpents. He is particularly aware of those persons and events which are joyous and life giving. Yet these gifts, for all the excitement and possibility they bring, are double-edged. They make him aware of the destructive presuppositions which direct his present attitudes and behaviors. He is a person who knows things must be sold, that cherished and secure worlds can prove deadly. And the selling must mean not only release but commitment to what was found. Above all, one must buy the future which God has given. The Christian who is sensitized by the parables understands the movement of God in his life through the patterns of finding, selling, and buying.

The Christian uses the pattern not only to detect the autobiographical movement of God but to discern the covert actions of grace in other stories. The Bible is the primary symbolical source for the Christian peoples. Yet in every age secondary symbols arise which are biblically influenced yet specifically geared to contemporary sensibilities. In the middle ages, Christ was imaged as a pelican who fed its children with its own blood. This image is not found in the Bible yet it is consonant with the biblical symbols of atonement and therefore an expression of Christian convictions. In a similar way contemporary storytelling can reflect the redemptive patterns present in the Bible. The stories of Flannery O'Connor are tales of parabolic reversal.[32] Her characters are rudely (and often lethally) shocked out of their destructive perspectives and offered a painful but healing new life. The Christian who applies the parabolic pattern to human experience can also look to contemporary stories and see there, beyond the surface secularity, the redemptive activity of God.

The most recent novel of Graham Greene, *The Honorary Counsel*, suggests a parabolic pattern of redemption. This is not a guess at Greene's intentions but an attempt to interpret the tale as a story of God. Charlie Fortnum is an honorary counsel (the lowest form of diplomatic life) for the

British Foreign Office. He is sixty-one, lives in a city in the north of Argentina, and does occasional favors (shows royalty the ruins) for the office in Buenos Aires. When the American Ambassador comes to visit the outlying province, Charley is asked to act as translator. A band of amateur revolutionaries led by an ex-priest, Fr. Leon Rivas, are plotting to kidnap the Ambassador and hold him in exchange for political prisoners. But instead of the highly negotiable American Ambassador they nab poor old drunken Charley. Nevertheless the ultimatum goes out: either the prisoners are released or Charley Fortnum dies.

The man who connects the revolutionaries and Charley and the central character of the novel is Dr. Eduardo Plarr. Plarr is Charley's drinking buddy and both doctor and lover to Clara, Charley's twenty-year-old wife. He is also the childhood friend of Fr. Leon and supplies the revolutionaries with information in the hope that his father will be among the prisoners released. The military eventually surround the hut where Fr. Leon and the revolutionaries are holding Fortnum. Plarr goes outside the hut to plead with Colonel Perez for more time and is shot. Fr. Leon rushes to Plarr's aid and is also cut down. The rest of the revolutionaries are either killed or captured leaving Charley Fortnum, days later, to reveal the meaning of the situation to Crichton, a smug member of the Foreign Service. Crichton remarks that the revoutionaries "had more luck than they deserved. They needn't have been caught up in things." Charley replies, "Perhaps it was love of a kind. People do get caught up by love, Crichton. Sooner or later."

Dr. Eduardo Plarr is a wasteland figure. Half-English, half-Paraguayan, his alienation is built into his biology. He leaves a lucrative practice in the Capital to minister in the barrios of a backwoods town, not out of a sense of social mission but because he is strangely pulled to the place where he last saw his father. He sleeps with other men's wives but with little enjoyment. He is neither tormented nor elated by his adulteries. Early in the story Plarr tells Fortnum, "The word love has never meant anything to me. Like the word God." The final hut scene reveals the full impact of this statement. Fr. Leon tells Plarr he is jealous of Charley Fortnum. "Jealous of Charley Fortnum? Why should I be jealous? Jealous because of the child?—but the child's mine. Jealous because of his wife? She's mine as well. For as long as I want her." The priest replies, "Jealous because he loves." It is Eduardo Plarr's moment of truth and the truth is devastatingly comic. "I know how to fuck—I don't know how to love. Poor drunken Charley Fortnum wins the games." It is after this that Plarr stands before the soldier's guns in an attempt to buy time for Charley and is murdered. Dr. Eduardo Plarr has come in out of the cold.

Dr. Plarr is deep in a situation of sin. He lives in a totally self-centered world and his energies

are spent in endless manipulations to protect it.
He hopes for some release by finding the strength
of his lost father. Instead he is jolted from his
non-caring world by the weakness of a man old
enough to be his father. The moments and car-
riers of grace are never what we expect them to
be. By all standards of society, Charley Fortnum
is pitiable. He is a strung-out failure who has
committed the unpardonable indiscretion of
marrying a twenty-year old whore. When he has
discovered he has been cuckolded and his cherished unborn child is really Plarr's, he cannot
even maintain rage. At the slightest hint that
Clara is capable of love (for her unborn child), he
accepts her back. In short he is vulnerable
enough to be the vehicle of grace, weak enough
for power to come to perfection. He is one of
Graham Greene's samaritans and tax collectors
who bear painful and laughing witness to radical
grace. It is this very "weakness" which permits
Charley to see the religious meaning of all that
has happened (and speak the novel's main metaphor). "There's nothing wrong in love, Clara. It
happens. It doesn't much matter who with. We
get caught up," he told her . . . "we get kid-
napped . . . by mistake." Plarr's find is sudden
and unbidden. Of all possible people, Charley
Fortnum penetrates to the center of his world and
overturns it. This find demands he sell the "taken
for granted" world that he is a winner and
Charley is a loser. "Poor drunken Charley wins
the game." Having sold the world of self-pre-

occupation, he must buy into the world of love.
He does this by risking himself to save Charley
and laying down his life for his friend. *The Honorary Counsel* is about people but parabolic
sensitivity sees that it is also a story of God. It is
a concrete tale of Eduardo Plarr's time of invitation and decision and so of the redemptive movement of God in his life.

The parables, whether functioning as metaphor
or simile, create a world of surprise but not
definite expectation, of suddenness but not intervention. At any given moment the strangest event
or the most unlikely people beckon to us, lure us
into new life. Two time honored Christian catch
phrases, "God sent you" and "You are Christ"
can be reinterpreted from this perspective. To
say to someone, "God must have sent you," is not
to imply that a third party, God, whispered in her
ear and she came. It means that her presence
precipitated the movement of God in you. She is a
graced opening out of the destructiveness you are
trapped in. In a similar way, to tell a person she is
Christ is not to suggest a mystical union but that
her presence functions as Jesus' did. She stirs up
the divine in your godless situation. Gracious
ambush is a way of life in the world of the
parables.

Yet this gracious world is also a dangerous
one. The parables are stories without alibis. The
excuse that "I knew you were a hard man so I
buried the money" is met with the rebuke, "If you
knew I was a hard man, you should have risked

the money." King Lear ridicules the idea of a
world where human freedom is not solely responsible: ". . . when we are sick in fortune . . .
we make guilty of our disasters the sun, the moon,
and the stars; as if we were villains by necessity,
fools by heavenly compulsion, knaves, thieves,
and teachers by spherical predominance, drunk-
ards, liars, and adulterers by an enforced obedi-
ence of planetary influence." The parables do not
allow this type of scapegoating. Christian drama
spotlights human decision making.

> To carry the drama over to the moral plane—this,
> however, was the task of Christianity. . . . It is a
> question of moral tragedy—of that kind which makes
> so momentous the text: 'If salt has lost its taste, how
> can its saltness be restored?' It is this kind of tragedy
> which concerns me.[33]

The parables hold to the paradox that a gracious
world is also perilous.

In the parables of Jesus, God is the plot. He is
what the people within the parables are undergoing or what the people hearing the parables
are undergoing. These stories of invitation and
decision both presuppose and witness to divine
activity. The activity is not a separate and discernible element of human life or parabolic storytelling. When through a graced person or event
people are shaken from the sinful destructiveness
they find themselves trapped in and offered new
life, God is present and active. In the stories
God's presence is acknowledged in the trans-

formation of human life. At times the parables
themselves function as the initiators of invitation
and decision. At other times we use the pattern
perceived in the parables to understand the
redemptive movements in our experiences and in
contemporary storytelling. In either case we are
in a world of invitation and decision.

The world of invitation and decision con-
cretizes the stories of hope and justice, trust and
freedom; and the stories of hope and justice,
trust and freedom support the world of invitation
and decision. The first two sets of stories create
convictions and values but do not investigate how
these are carried out in actual life. Hope, justice,
trust, and freedom are not static ideals but a
redemptive process enacted in a world of invitation and decision. In a way, the stories of
hope and justice, trust and freedom are the
content of God and the story of invitation and
decision is the form. On the other hand, the
world of invitation and decision can appear
unyielding. There is a purging aspect to the
redemptive process which the parables do not
shy away from. The halting, never-ending movement from sin to redemption would paralyze and
debilitate us if we did not tell the other stories.
From these stories we know that the Mystery is
love and that the conversion process, no matter
how painful, is the way of our well-being. All
three of these tales, therefore, merge into a
single story of God. and, of course, God's story is
ours.

NOTES

Chapter One

1. E. H. Erickson, *Young Man Luther: A Study in Psychoanalysis and History* (New York: W. N. Norton & Co., 1958), pp. 21-22.

2. Nikos Kazantzakis, *Report to Greco* (New York: Simon & Schuster, 1976), p. 291.

3. This list is not meant to be taxative. Perhaps the most obvious omission is the human person's relationship to the machines he has manufactured.

4. Bernard Malamud, *The Fixer* (New York, Pocket Books), p. 45.

5. Quoted in E. Mark Stern and Bert G. Marino, *Psychotheology* (New York: Newman Press, 1970), p. 2.

6. Langdon Gilkey, *Naming the Whirlwind* (Indianapolis: Bobbs-Merrill, 1969), p. 296.

7. This quote is a combination of two different descriptive versions of Heidegger. The first part of the quote is from "The Origin of the Work of Art," in *Poetry, Language, Thought* (New York: Harper & Row, 1971), pp. 33-34. The second part of the quote is from "Art and Being," in *Art and Philosophy* (New York, 1966), p. 172.

8. Mircea Eliade, *The Forge and the Crucible* (New York: Harper & Row, Publishers, 1962), p. 143.

9. Quoted in F. David Martin, "The Aesthetic in Religious Experience," *Religious Studies* (October, 1968), p. 13.

10. Hannah Arendt, *The Human Condition* (New York: Doubleday & Co., 1958), p. 3.

11. Quoted in F. David Martin, "The Beautiful as Symbolic of the Holy," *The Christian Scholar*, Vol. XLI, No. 2 (June, 1958), p. 129.

12. Cf. Gilkey, *Whirlwind*, 315-330.

13. Quoted in Martin, "Beautiful,"

14. Cf. Gregory Baum, *Man Becoming* (New York: Herder and Herder, 1970), Chpt. 2.

15. Par Lagerkvist, "My Father and I," *The Marriage Feast* (New York: Farrar, Straus and Giroux, 1954), pp. 33-34.

16. Sam D. Gill, "Disenchantment," *Parabola*, Vol. 1 (Spring, 1976), p. 9.

17. Cf. Noel Dermot O'Donoghue, "Response as a Human Dimension," *The New Scholasticism* (Winter, 1972), p. 187.

18. Quoted in S. Paul Schelling, *God Incognito* (Nashville: Abingdon Press, 1974), pp. 81-82.

Chapter Two

1. Gordon Kaufman, *The Problem of God* (Cambridge, Mass.: Harvard University Press, 1972), p. 100.

2. Alan Watts, *Beyond Theology: The Art of Godmanship* (New York: Pantheon Books, 1964), p. 29.

3. Clifford Geertz, "Religion as a Cultural System," in *The Religious Situation* 1968, Donald R. Cutler, ed. (Boston: Beacon Press, 1968), p. 663.

4. Quoted in Van A. Harvey, *The Historian and the Believer* (Toronto: The Macmillan Co., 1966), p. 256.

5. Pierre Teilhard de Chardin, *The Divine Milieu* (New York: Harper & Row), p. 61.

6. Nathan A. Scott, Jr. *Negative Capability* (New Haven: Yale University Press, 1969), p. xiv.

7. Charles Davis, *Temptations of Religious* (New York: Harper & Row, Publishers, 1973), Chapter 1.

8. Langdon Gilkey, "Modern Myth-Making and the Possibilities of Twentieth Century Theology." Theology of Renewal, Vol. I, ed. by L. K. Shook (Montreal: Palm Publishers, 1968).

9. Quoted in Herbert Weisinger, *The Agony and the Triumph* (East Lansing, Michigan: Michigan State University Press, 1964), p. 200.

10. Quoted in Frederick Ferre, *Shaping The Future* (New York: Harper & Row, 1976), p. 11.

11. Sheldon B. Kopp, *If You Meet the Buddha on the Road, Kill Him!* (Ben Lomond, California: Science and Behavior Books, Inc., 1972), p. 31.

12. Donald D. Evans, *The Logic of Self-Involvement* (London: SCM Press, 1963), p. 158.

13. Nikos Kazantzakis, *Report to Greco* (New York: Simon and Schuster, 1965), p. 292.

14. Sam Keen, *To a Dancing God* (New York: Harper & Row, Publishers, 1970).

15. Elie Wiesel, *Messengers of God* (New York: Random House, 1976), p. 97.

16. Amos Wilder, *The New Voice* (New York: Herder and Herder, 1969), p. 54, 70.

17. Quoted in Wilder, p. 54.

18. Langdon Gilkey, *Religion and the Scientific Future* (New York: Harper & Row, 1970), p. 97.

19. Elie Wiesel, *The Oath* (New York: Avon, 1970), p. 11.

20. E. Linnemann. Quoted in Norman Perrin, *Rediscovering the Teaching of Jesus* (New York: Harper & Row, 1967), p. 118.

21. Harald Weinrich, "Narrative Theology" in *The Crisis of Religious Language*, eds., Johann Metz and Jean-Pierre Jossua (New York: Herder and Herder, 1973), p. 53.

22. Nikos Kazantzakis, *Saint Francis* (New York: Simon and Schuster, 1962), p. 231.

23. Quoted in Andrew Greeley, *The New Agenda* (New York: Doubleday & Co., 1973), p. 64.

24. Paul Ricoeur, The Symbolism of Evil (Boston: Beacon Press, 1967), p. 35.

25. Cf. ibid., 354. "The world of symbols is not a tranquil and reconciled world; every symbol is iconoclastic in comparison with some other symbol, just as every symbol, left to itself, tends to *thicken*, to become solidified in an idolatry." (emphasis mine)

26. John Knox, *The Humanity and Divinity of Christ* (Cambridge: Cambridge University Press, 1967), p. 106-107.

Chapter Three

1. George Orwell, *1984*. (New York: Signet Books, 1950), p. 200.

2. Claus Westermann, "The Way of the Promise through the Old Testament" in *The Old Testament and Christian Faith*, ed. by Bernhard W. Anderson (New York, Harper and Row, 1963), p. 207.

3. Rosemary Radford Ruether, *The Radical Kingdom* (New York: Harper & Row, Publishers, 1970), p. 9.

4. Jurgen Moltmann, *Theology of Hope* (New York: Harper & Row, Publishers, 1965), p. 51.

5. S. G. F. Brandon, *Jesus and the Zealots* (New York: Charles Scribner's Sons, 1967), p. 51.

6. H. McCabe, *Law, Love, and Language* (New York: Sheed and Ward, 1968), p. 133. Quoted in J. B. Davies, *Christians, Politics and Violent Revolution* (New York: Orbis Books, 1976), p. 104.

7. J. G.Davies, *Christian, Politics and Violent Revolution* (New York: Orbis Books, 1976), p. 100.

8. Leszek Kolakowski, "Der revolutionare Geist." Quoted in *The Apocalyptic Movement* Walter Schmithals, trans. by John E. Steely (New York: Abingdon Press, 1975), p. 248.

9. B. Albrektson, *History and the Gods* (Lund, 1967).

10. James Barr, "Story and History in Biblical Theology," *Journal of Religion* (January, 1976), p. 16.

11. Gerhard von Rad, *Old Testament Theology*, Vol. I (New York: Harper & Row, Publishers, 1962), p. 231.

12. Abraham Heschel, *The Prophets* Vol. 1 (New York: Harper Torchbooks, 1962), p. 198.

13. William A. Beardslee, *Literary Criticism of the New Testament* (Philadelphia, Fortress Press, 1970), p. 54.

Chapter Four

1. Cf. Gordon Kaufman, *Systematic Theology: A Historicist Perspective* (New York: Charles Scribner's Sons, 1968), pp. 190-209.

2. Sam Keen, *To a Dancing God* (New York: Harper & Row, 1970), p. 130. Quoted in John F. Haught, *Religion and Self-Acceptance* (New York: Paulist Press, 1976), pp. 166-67.

3. Herbert Richardson, *Toward An American Theology* (New York: Harper & Row, 1967), pp. 157-58.

4. Gerhard von Rad, *Old Testament Theology*, Vol. I (New York: Harper & Row, 1962), p. 148.

5. Richardson, 123-126. Richardson also investigates dignity as the basis of authority.

6. Richardson, p. 126.

7. Richardson, p. 147.

8. Gerard Manley Hopkins.

9. Gerhard von Rad, *Old Testament Theology*, Vol. I (New York: Harper & Row, 1962), p. 149.

10. Walter Brueggermann, *In Man We Trust* (Atlanta: John Knox Press, 1972), p. 44.

11. Brueggermann, p. 35.

12. Bruggermann, p. 36.

13. Cf. Andrew Greeley, *The New Agenda* (New York: Doubleday & Co., 1973), Chapter Five.

14. Cf. Claus Westermann, *Creation* (Philadelphia: Fortress Press, 1974), p. 92.

15. John Updike, *Couples* (New York: Fawcett Publications, 1968), p. 255.

16. H. R. Riebuhr, *Radical Monotheism and Western Culture* (New York: Harper & Row, 1960), p. 28. Quoted in Norman Young, *Creator, Creation, and Faith* (Philadelphia, The Westminster Press, 1976), p. 57.

17. Gerhard von Rad, *Wisdom in Israel* (New York: Abingdon Press, 1972), p. 194.

18. Elie, Wiesel, *Night*, Trans. by Stella Rodway (New York: Hill and Wang, 1960), pp. 70f.

19. Herbert Fingarette, *Self-Deception* (London: Routledge and Kegan Paul, 1969), p. 47f. Quoted in Haught, p. 152.

20. James Mackay, *Problems of Religious Faith* (Chicago: Franciscan Herald Press, 1972), p. 195.

21. The Cross, of course, can be considered as a "turning point" in history as it is in many theologies. It is debatable whether the Fall can be considered as a historical event.

Chapter Five

1. Lawrence Durrell, *Monsieur* (New York: Pocket Books), pp. 183-84.

2. Delmore Schwartz, quoted by Stanley Romaine Hopper, "The Poetry of Meaning" in *Literature and Religion* (New York: Harper Forum Books), p. 227.

3. Rudolf Bultmann, *Jesus Christ and Mythology* (London: SCM), p. 19.

4. Brian Wicker, *The Story-Shaped World* (Notre Dame, Indiana: University of Notre Dame Press, 1975), p. 103.

5. Walter Brueggemann, "On Trust and Freedom," *Interpretation*, Vol. XXVI (1972), p. 18.

6. Nikos Kazantzakis, *Report to Greco* (New York: Simon and Schuster, 1965), p. 234.

7. Martin Buber, "Faith of Judaism," *Israel and the World*, p. 22.

8. Norman Perrin, *Jesus and the Language of the Kingdom* (Philadelphia: Fortress Press, 1976), p. 202.

9. Amos Niven Wilder, *Theopoetic* (Philadelphia: Fortress Press, 1976), p. 77.

10. Cf. Ray Hart, *Unfinished Man and the Imagination* (New York: Herder and Herder, 1968), p. 259.

11. Norman Perrin, *Rediscovering the Teaching of Jesus* (New York: Harper & Row, Publishers, 1967), p. 5.

12. This account of models of divine activity follows the outline of Ian G. Barbour, *Myths, Models and Paradigms* (New York: Harper & Row, Publishers, 1974), pp. 155-170.

13. David Griffin, "Is Revelation Coherent?" *Theology Today*, Vol. XXVIII (October, 1971), p. 293.

14. David Mackay, *The Problems of Religious Faith* (Chicago: Franciscan Herald Press, 1972).

15. Ibid., p. 85.

16. Ibid., p. 87.

17. Ibid., p. 95.

18. Ibid., p. 201.

19. Ibid., pp. 183-84.

20. Ibid., p. 192.

21. Dominic Crossan, *The Dark Interval* (Chicago: Argus Press, 1975), pp. 72-77.

22. Robert Funk, *Language, Hermeneutic, and Word of God* (New York: Harper & Row, Publishers, 1966), p. 18.

23. Cf. Perrin, *Jesus*, pp. 89-193. This work of Perrin is a guide to parable research.

24. Ibid., p. 179.

25. Dominic Crossan, *In Parables* (New York: Harper & Row, Publishers, 1973), p. 64.

26. Funk, p. 214. Quoted in Perrin, *Jesus*, p. 139.

27. Quoted in Perrin, *Jesus*, p. 178.

28. Cf. Robert C. Tannehill, *The Sword of His Mouth* (Philadelphia: Fortress Press, 1975).

29. Crossan, *Parables*, p. 83.

30. Hart, *Imagination*, p. 278.

31. Crossan, *Parables*, pp. 34-36.

32. Cf. John R. May, *The Pruning Word* (Notre Dame, Indiana: Notre Dame Press, 1976).

33. Andre Gide. Quoted in Amos Wilder, *Early Christian Rhetoric* (Cambridge, Mass.: Harvard University Press, 1971), p. 76.